How To
Shorten Your Job Search

GARY CALVANESO

Copyright © 2018 Gary Calvaneso

All rights reserved.

ISBN: 1721624872
ISBN-13: 978-1721624874

Contents

ACKNOWLEDGEMENTS v
FORWARD vii
Chapter 1 11
LEARNING THE JOB SEARCH PROCESS 11
Chapter 2 15
YOU'RE UNEMPLOYED – NOW WHAT? 15
Chapter 3 26
MANAGING YOUR FINANCES THROUGH A JOB
TRANSITION 26
Chapter 4 35
DECIDING WHAT YOU WANT TO DO NEXT 35
Chapter 5 59
DEVELOPING YOUR PERSONAL BRAND............................59
Chapter 6 82
CREATE YOUR SELF-MARKETING TOOLS 82
Chapter 7 86
HOW TO WRITE A WINNING RESUME 86
Chapter 8 143
COVER LETTERS THAT GET ATTENTION........................143
Chapter 9 158
USING LINKEDIN IN YOUR JOB SEARCH 158
Chapter 10 181
TARGETING COMPANIES 181
Chapter 11 199
GET OUT THERE AND NETWORK! 199
Chapter 12 222
WORKING WITH RECRUITERS 222
Chapter 13 231
WINNING THE JOB INTERVIEW 231
Chapter 14 258
SALARY NEGOCIATION 258
ABOUT THE AUTHOR 276

GARY CALVANESO

HOW TO
SHORTEN YOUR JOB SEARCH

A PROVEN APPROACH TO LANDING A POSITION

GARY CALVANESO

ACKNOWLEDGEMENTS

I would like to first thank my wife Diana for her encouragement and support in writing this book. I would also like to thank the many volunteers at Saddleback's Career Coaching and Counseling Ministry for their dedication to helping others as well as their inputs and support in the development of the career coaching curriculum.

As a member of Saddleback's Career Coaching and Counseling, I cannot express the personal reward I received each time I learned that I had helped someone be successful in an interview because of something they learned in one of my sessions. I am very proud to have been a part of this ministry and to have led the development of the curriculum.

The Saddleback Career Coaching Ministry has been one of the largest of its kind in Southern California and each week it coaches many professional, experienced, unemployed people who seek help and guidance on what to do next in their career. The ministry provides the course materials and instruction to teach candidates strategies and techniques to improve their job search skills. More importantly, they teach the value of having faith, helping others and believing in yourself.

About Saddleback Church

If you are not familiar with Saddleback Church, Pastor Rick Warren has written the "Purpose Driven Life", which has sold over 32 million copies in more than 85 languages. Over the years, Pastor Rick has helped me understand my purpose here on earth, which is to serve others. His teachings inspired me to write this book.

FORWARD

Whether you've decided it's time to make a career change or are currently unemployed, this book is designed to help you manage the process of job transition. While some of the content of this book may apply to non-professional roles, it is primarily focused on those that are seeking professional positions in startup, small, midsize or large companies.

We'll explore a number of areas including; *how to find the right job for you, how to market yourself, how to deal with job transition, what to do if you've lost your job and how to minimize the amount of time you are in transition.* While I cannot provide you with a job, I will guide you through a proven job search methodology that can work for you.

How do I know? As a veteran of job transition, I speak from firsthand experience. I have personally used this same methodology to successfully locate and obtain a number of corporate positions in different industries.

During my professional career, I changed industries a number of times. These industries include teaching, medical device, asset tracking, computer manufacturing, aerospace and defense, as well as oil and gas. Through my own transition experience and by learning from others, I have developed a number of job search techniques and put them all together in an easy to follow process.

For nearly 9 years, I am proud to have helped hundreds of job seekers at Saddleback Career Coaching & Counseling and was responsible for developing and leading the career coaching curriculum. Much of the content of this book is based on the course material and structure I developed and used for the Saddleback Career Coaching and Counseling curriculum. Over the years, this material has been taught to thousands of people, many of whom have acknowledged that it has helped them find their next position and shorten their job search. **Here is one of them.**

Robert's Story

Robert was frustrated that he was getting interviews but had not been hired. Since Robert was able to find positions in his field and was getting interviews, it was very evident that he was doing a good job marketing himself and his resume / LinkedIn profile was appealing to potential employers. It was clear that his issue was not with his marketing, but with his interview skills.

I walked Robert through a "mock" interview to gauge his responses to a number of standard questions. While Robert did a good job communicating his skill set in writing on his resume, his verbal responses to my questions showed he was unprepared.

I asked Robert to explain how he prepares for each interview. Robert's response was *"I get ready to do a lot of selling but since I don't know what the employer will ask me, there's not much to prepare for"*. It was evident from his answer that the root cause of his interview performance was a lack of preparation and not understanding what employers are really looking for during an interview.

As we'll discuss in a later chapter on interviewing, I explained to Robert that when you reach the interview stage, the employer has <u>already determined</u> that you are qualified for the job. The interview discussion is not actually about selling yourself. It is about showing that you are relative and "fit" within the company culture. During the interview, you will need to communicate that you are the candidate who is capable of handling the responsibilities of the position. While you are having a dialogue, the interviewer will be analyzing your personality, attitude and demeanor asking themselves; *"do I feel comfortable / can I work with this person"?*

Like Robert, many job seekers think that succeeding in an interview is all about the ability to sell themselves. An interview is not the place to bring up a lot of irrelevant jobs or experiences that you have had during your lifetime. You don't have to be the smartest person, nor do you need to meet every qualification on the job description, you just need to "fit".

To summarize this point about interviewing, I told Robert to remember;

It is not the smartest person or the most qualified that gets the job; it's the person that interviews the best!

In other words, it is the person that does the best job convincing the employer that he or she is the best candidate that *fits the needs of the job* that will get you hired. You don't need to check every box on the job description to be qualified or have the exact experience listed.

I suggested to Robert that he needed to do a great deal of preparation before an interview. This includes understanding the needs of the company and mapping out where his skill set matches those requested on job description. He also needed to practice his interview responses to be able to articulate the strong points of his skills and experience and to explain how they relate to the job. Once he understood the process and was able to communicate how his skills matched the needs of the position, he was hired after his next interview!

Understanding the Transition Process

Through my experience as a career coach, I have learned that too many job seekers don't understand how to create and use personal marketing to get employers to find them. Many candidates simply create a LinkedIn profile and spend the majority of their time sitting at home on their computer sending resumes to positions listed on websites such as Indeed.com, Craigslist, Careerbuilder.com, and other on-line job sites, hoping someone will notice.

For every job posted, these sites receive hundreds if not thousands of resumes. Given that level of competing applicants, they are not the most effective way for you to land a job. This is not to say that no one ever gets hired. For professional positions, the probability of landing through these job sites is lower and takes longer.

Ask yourself:

- *Is your job search strategy sitting on the computer sending resumes to on-line job sites?*
- *Are you getting few if any responses by sending out your resume?*
- *Are you getting interviews, but not getting hired?*
- *Do you believe you are not getting a job because of your age or lack of experience*
- *How can you stand out from the rest of the crowd of job seekers?*
- *Why have others landed that are less qualified than you?*
- *How can you stand out from the rest of the crowd of job seekers?*

If any of these questions relate to your personal situation, this book is designed to teach you how to shorten the time it takes to land a position.

Best of luck in your job search!

Step 1
Develop Job Transition Strategy — Understanding The Job Search Process

Chapter 1

LEARNING THE JOB SEARCH PROCESS

A Step by Step Approach

Let's begin by defining the process steps that can help you *shorten your job search*.

In the following chapters, we will thoroughly cover each of these steps and provide the details to land your next position. As we move through the process, you will notice that I refer to related information in other chapters whenever they connect to the subject matter. This is to reinforce their importance and to keep you focused on making each personal decision for career direction, goals and needs. Only you can decide on where you want to focus your job search.

In this book, I will provide a wealth of information on various search methods, developing job search tools that work, how to effectively conduct an interview and how to negotiate your salary. So, let's get started!

The Job Search Process

There are *5 functional steps* involved in the job search process as shown in the chart below:

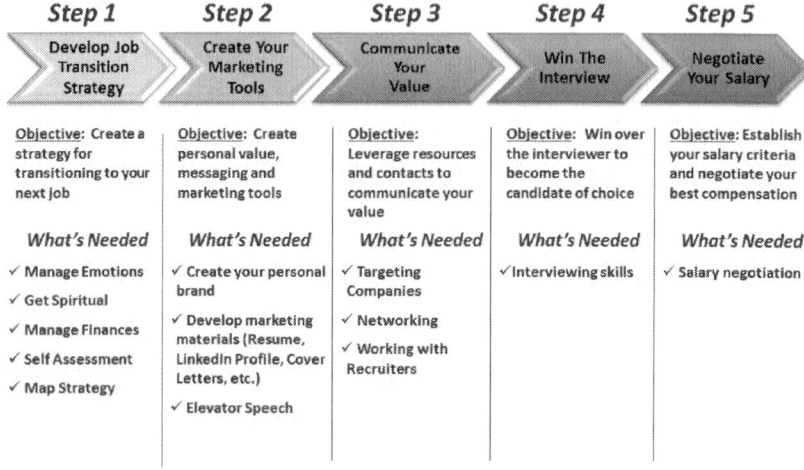

Figure 1-1: The Job Search Process

You'll notice that within each step is a series of activities and tools required as part of the step. While the descriptions below are a simplified overview of each process step, other chapters in this book will provide you with all the details.

Step 1. *Develop your job search transition strategy* – The first step is to get yourself ready to move forward, especially getting your finances in order. You'll need to conduct a self-assessment, decide what position you are seeking and get organized. You should also find an accountability partner to help you stay focused.

Step 2. *Create your marketing and tools* - From your self-assessment and career direction; you'll create a summary of what skills and experience make you valuable to a prospective employer. This will help you emphasize what makes you stand out from the rest of the crowd. Your "value" can then be marketed to potential employers as your "personal brand".

Once you have created your personal brand, you'll use it to develop consistent messaging that goes into all your marketing materials. These materials include your resume, your LinkedIn profile, biography, etc. To be able to communicate what you offer when you meet others in person, you'll also need to develop a "sales pitch" to quickly convey your value in a short, succinct manner. Keep in mind that the largest percentage of your search process will be focused on marketing yourself.

Step 3. *Communicate your value* – Once you've created the marketing tools that support your "value", you'll need get out there and communicate your "brand" to others. As part of this step, you'll need to make a list of companies that you would like to work for. In another chapter, we will discuss how to effectively network your way into a job at one of the companies you've listed.

We'll also discuss how to effectively network to meet others that could open doors for you. Networking, both in person and online, is a very important part of communicating your value to others.

Step 4. *Win the interview* – It takes a great deal of effort and preparation just to reach the interview stage. When you finally get there, it is critical that you understand what is required to be successful in an interview. It's highly unlikely that you are the only candidate applying, so you not only need to make a good impression, but also need to communicate that you are a better fit for the company.

Step 5. *Negotiate your value* – Once you are offered the position, there will be a brief opportunity to negotiate your salary and benefits. As a general rule, the higher the level of position, the greater the opportunity to tactfully negotiate salary and benefits. In the end, your salary determines your spending power, so this is an important step in the process regardless of the level of position.

Chapter 2

YOU'RE UNEMPLOYED – NOW WHAT?

If you believe you are about to be terminated or have lost your job and are unemployed; this chapter applies to you. If you are considering making a career change, and especially if you are disillusioned in your current job, there is some important information that we will cover, particularly about attitude. Making a career change because you feel you are going nowhere, are bored in your job or have been passed over for a promotion are good reasons to get your attitude in check BEFORE you quit and start looking for another job.

Keep in mind changing jobs, lay-offs, outsourcing, and hiring freezes are all part of working in "Corporate America". Changes occur even in the best of economic times. Regardless of the reason, when you become unemployed, you face the reality that your monthly bills are still there and will probably be asking yourself; what should I do now? Start by taking a deep breath and don't panic.

Shock and Awe

If you are part of a layoff, the news that you are no longer going to be employed can be devastating. A typical response is to feel dejected or to think we've failed in the job and there's a natural tendency is to run away from the problem and hibernate. The truth is; very talented people are also caught up in layoffs.

The loss of a job is usually caused by one of several possible reasons; a downturn in business, a lack of cash flow, internal restructuring, sale of the company or something else. It is also possible that you've lost your job due to your lack of personal performance, personality conflict with your boss or something you did that violated company policy or the law. Unless you are the only employee terminated, the actual cause of your job loss may have nothing to do with your performance or with you personally.

What to do

While there is no easy way to prepare yourself for termination, careful planning can make a definite impact on your how fast you recover. As soon as you learn that you will no longer be employed, meet with your human resources department to discuss the details of termination benefits or a possible severance package. The type and depth of package will of course depend on the level of position that you have.

Even though there is a natural tendency to run away, <u>do the opposite and stick around</u> to negotiate the terms of your departure. This action could result in a better overall severance package because employers have feelings too. Let's face it, managers are not delighted to send out layoff notices either. It is difficult for anyone to tell an employee that their job and income has just been eliminated. While there are always exceptions, most managers are vulnerable during this time and will likely be more willing to do something for you. This remorse lasts a very short time because once you are gone, they will move on. The more time that goes by, the less likely they will be willing to help. Be aggressive and don't wait to ask!

At the time of termination of employment:

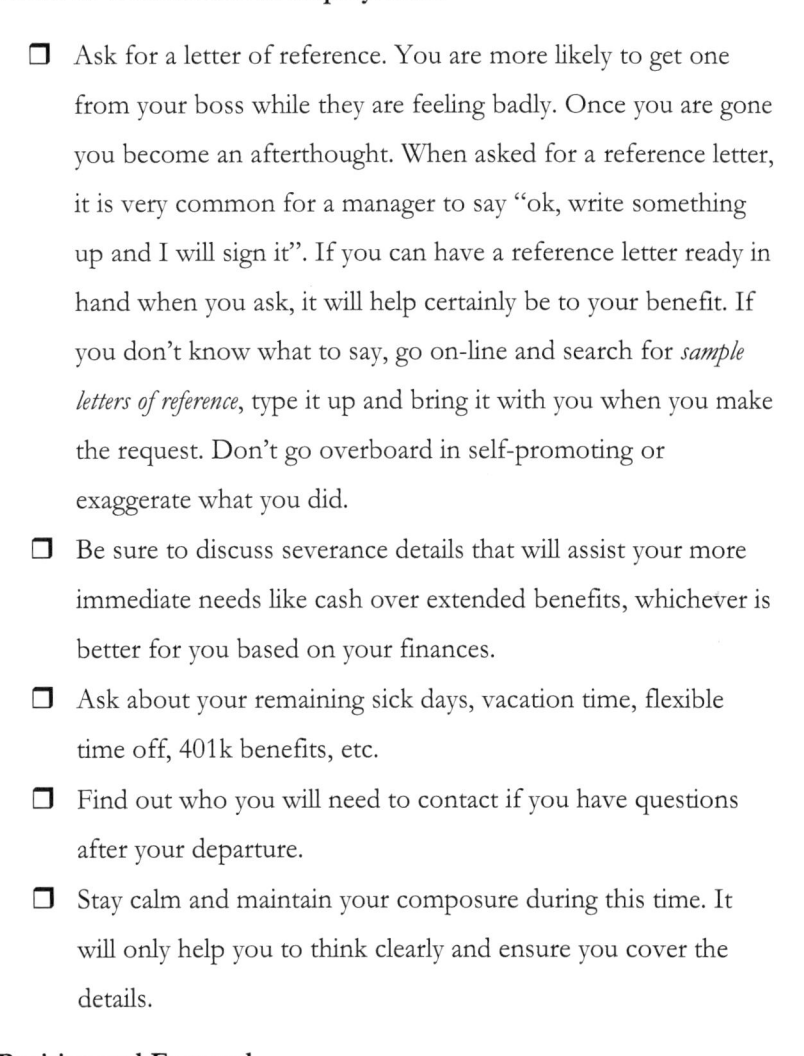

- ❒ Ask for a letter of reference. You are more likely to get one from your boss while they are feeling badly. Once you are gone you become an afterthought. When asked for a reference letter, it is very common for a manager to say "ok, write something up and I will sign it". If you can have a reference letter ready in hand when you ask, it will help certainly be to your benefit. If you don't know what to say, go on-line and search for *sample letters of reference*, type it up and bring it with you when you make the request. Don't go overboard in self-promoting or exaggerate what you did.
- ❒ Be sure to discuss severance details that will assist your more immediate needs like cash over extended benefits, whichever is better for you based on your finances.
- ❒ Ask about your remaining sick days, vacation time, flexible time off, 401k benefits, etc.
- ❒ Find out who you will need to contact if you have questions after your departure.
- ❒ Stay calm and maintain your composure during this time. It will only help you to think clearly and ensure you cover the details.

Stay Positive and Focused

Keep things in perspective. If you have decided to quit your job because you are disillusioned or think you can do better somewhere else, stay humble and be professional when you leave. As you sever ties, your attitude will determine your altitude! If you have be laid off, it is natural to feel angry or feel like you should get even, but don't. It will buy you nothing.

Keep this in mind; if you're qualified and are a hard worker, you will find another job. You just need to know the process of how to locate an opportunity and how to land it.

Never Take A Job Just To Have One

There is a simple reason why employers reject people that are over qualified. They recognize that you'll end up leaving when something better comes along. When you job hop, your resume may show patterns of rapid job turnover and/ or indicates the level of position you are currently employed in has gone backward. Employers get concerned when a resume shows very short stays or when candidates move from higher level jobs to lower level ones.

The lesson here is not to take any job just because you need one. If you do, you may find yourself underpaid, frustrated or dissatisfied. Work on getting your emotions in check and you'll be able to focus on landing the job you really want. Take this opportunity of transition to align your interests and abilities with the type of work you would enjoy doing every day.

Emotional Grief

The reason I focused this chapter on this subject is to *emphasize the importance of getting your emotions in check*! Career coaches say that a key part of the job search is a process of managing your own emotions. You must focus on controlling your thoughts and emotions in a way that will serve you positively.

As we will discuss later in this book, one of the key things employers are looking for in an interview will be to determine how well you "fit" in the company culture. It is important that you are able to keep your emotions in check because an unhappy person doesn't fit in anyone's corporate culture. Carrying bitterness and resentment can eat you up inside and it may show during an interview. This is especially true when someone speaks negatively about his or her last boss or company. NO ONE will hire an unhappy person!

Manage Your Stress

The prospect of finding a new job can be overwhelming and stressful especially in balancing the search with everything else going on in life. If you are stressed out while you are looking, it can make you look desperate to a potential employer. I have seen candidates beg for a job during the interview, even pleading hardship. Begging shows unstable emotion and will hurt your chances of getting hired.

Life is Not All About Your Job

What is very important for your mental focus is to keep things in perspective because what you are is NOT defined by your career. If you believe your job defines who you are, you will be unfulfilled when you lose it. Separate yourself from your job. A job is some place you travel to and lend your skills, but it doesn't make you any more or less valuable as a person.

Be positive about who you already are and remember you do not need a career to validate yourself. If you fall into the worry rut and feel lousy about who you are, take time off from the search. Searching for a job is a full-time effort and like a regular job, sometimes requires a vacation to get re-energized.

Be Grateful

Instead of dwelling on the negative, look at the bright side. There is so much to be thankful for. Living in the United States, one of the wealthiest countries in the world, is a blessing.

To put this in perspective, through my church, I know of a company that provides back packs for children in third world countries. They fill them with basic utensils such as a hair brush, a tooth brush and sandals. The company donates them to very poor children in Africa and other 3rd world countries. These children get very excited to receive these basic items and react as if they won a lottery. They are so humble and ever so grateful because it is relative to their standard of living.

To those of us living in a great country like the United States, it is difficult to grasp the level of poverty these children live in. By comparison, many "poor" people in the U.S. have cell phones and HD flat screen televisions. The point here is if you never found a job again, you would probably never be as poor as those in some third world countries, so be grateful!

While it is sometimes a challenge to stay away from moods swing and depressing emotions, it is not a good idea to stay totally away from your emotions. Emotions can become your strength if you look put the situation in perspective and think clearly. Think of your situation as temporary and focus your emotions believing that this change is for the best, you can channel the negative energy into positive energy.

Get Involved with Others

Don't try to tackle your emotional job loss stress alone. Participate in a job search group as there are job search groups everywhere. Google your area and industry and you will most certainly locate several groups that you can network with. There are others out there going through the same emotional issues that you are and communicating with them is a way of controlling the stress. Try to schedule a lunch or a coffee once a week with someone for "informational exchanges".

Most importantly consider this, according to a LinkedIn survey, 85% of all jobs were filled via networking of some sort! We'll discuss these "networking" opportunities in a later chapter. However, the idea of networking is to learn about and help others. Through networking, you will gain valuable knowledge and insight to help make connections at specific companies you'd like to work for.

Consider Volunteering

You may want to consider a volunteer opportunity. Volunteering helps develop social skills and provides an opportunity to do something positive as part of a community. It is another method of networking and it avoids isolation and negative thinking.

Too often when job seekers feel stressed, they isolate themselves so developing a good social network is positive therapy and a coping mechanism. At the same time it expands your network. Ask for introductions and make cold calls. Use contacts wherever you find them. Participate in chamber of commerce activities, professional organizations and online forums. The important thing to note here is the fact that a high percentage of positions are found in the "hidden job market" (jobs that are internal or not posted) and they happen by networking with others.

Find an Accountability Partner – Your family and friends know this is a difficult time for you. Use your time wisely and communicate with those that care about you. It is a good idea to surround yourself with support. Find an accountably partner that will work together with you to give you honest feedback as you are making your decisions.

Exercise

It is important that you feel good about yourself during career transition. Don't let the search process become all consuming. Stress can have a physical impact on us that's not favorable and exercise is a good way to relieve it. Exercise every day to get your blood pumping to your brain and relieve the stress. Eat well and get plenty of rest. Go for a walk, try meditation techniques.

Think about what is working in your life. If you have good health, strong family relations and/or good friends, these are all positive things to be thankful for. When we focus on positive things that are working, we feel better. Put it all in perspective and have faith. <u>A job merely provides you with a place you work; it is not your life!</u>

Don't Procrastinate

Don't wait for the dust to settle, start planning your next steps. Don't delay the things you need to do by telling yourself, "I'll start tomorrow". Tomorrow will simply turn into the next day, then the next day and so on.

When you are stressed, it is easy to fall in the trap of spending loads of time work around the house or on useless tasks. A very common reaction is to sit in front of a computer, surf the web and apply for jobs on employment websites.

Use this transition time wisely to figure out where you want to go next in your career. When you come across a position of interest that you feel you are qualified for, go after it. Make your job search your total priority and focus. Spend your time searching and networking.

Use Your Time Wisely

It's easy to fall into a routine of sending your resume to every job that you see on-line. While at first this may make you feel like you're making some progress, applying on-line is generally ineffective and will frustrate you when the results don't happen. Think carefully about internet links and job postings that appear to be a good match for you. Searching the job boards and filling out applications is reactive. If you find a posting that looks like a fit, do the research on the company and determine if you truly believe you could provide value before investing the time to pursue it further.

Start a Routine

Fear is the emotion that often makes you feel that your current situation is out of control. Always remember that you are really in control of what you do.

Set personal goals that will focus your attention on actions. An effective technique is to set daily, weekly and monthly goals and develop and maintain a set schedule to ensure you are using your time wisely. Outline a daily, weekly and monthly action plan based on your goals and spend at least eight hours focused on your search if you're unemployed or two to three hours if you're currently employed. That's right. I am talking about *full time*.

Get Out There

The adage, "It's not what you know, but who you know," is not just a saying, it's a reality. When you work from home, it can get depressing being in the same location every day, especially when you are not getting the results you want. Find an alternate place that you can work; a library, a coffee shop, a church campus etc. Spend time meeting with others and network a few days a week. By moving around, you'll stay focused on the search process and are less likely to fall into the emotional traps of self-doubt. You won't know which contact, friend or colleague may be able to lead you to an upcoming interview. Don't sit behind the computer! Balance your job search activities by making it a point to network every single week.

Stay Organized

There is no excuse for clutter and disorganization. Make sure you have the important documents up to date and readily available. This includes letters of reference, awards, resumes, etc. Keep your schedule handy and make sure your workspace is clutter free. Getting organized will allow you to take charge of your search and will help relieve the pressure in preparing for upcoming interviews or phone calls with employers.

Monitor Your Progress

Measure your progress against your goals because you won't be as effective if you don't measure what you are doing. Monitoring your progress helps determine what aspects of your job search are working and helps to evaluate areas that could use improvement. Focus on the tasks that you are controlling, such as the hours you spend researching companies, the number of resumes you send out and where you sent them, networking events you attend, etc. Set realistic goals and reward yourself each time you achieve a small milestone. When you monitor where you are in your search and take pride in your accomplishments, it will reduce stress and keep you motivated to continue!

Be Patient

The job search process takes time, especially in a competitive industry or in a challenging market. It is very easy to become frustrated when we don't see any results. Keep in mind that employers move at their own pace which is usually <u>much slower</u> than yours. Even though you are in a hurry to get back to work, employers prefer to take the time to hire the right person. Stay focused and be patient as the process may take longer than you expect.

Focus on Your Faith – Seek spiritual guidance in your job search. When you lose your job, it's not only income that is lost but also a sense of meaning and this has a spiritual dimension. Seeking spiritual guidance and comfort is an effective way to ease the fear and panic associated with the loss of a job.

During your time in transition, take the time to give yourself to comfort others in similar situations. You will find it rewarding and you will be blessed.

Keep in mind that faith-based groups provide rich networking opportunities. When other networkers share a church or a faith, they are more likely to trust each other and will often go the extra mile for you. While God won't give you a reference, he can give strength and so much more if you ask for help and guidance.

Step 1: Develop Job Transition Strategy — Managing Your Finances

Chapter 3

MANAGING YOUR FINANCES THROUGH A JOB TRANSITION

Whether you have decided to quit your job before you have another one or have lost your job and are now unemployed, you are going to need to manage your finances. Regardless of the reason, your monthly payments are going to be there. It is important to analyze your personal situation and plan how to manage your financials during the transition. You've probably heard the expression that "cash is king". The reality of this truth will really set in when you find yourself living without a regular paycheck. For the analysis, let's start by looking at your expenses.

Step 1: Manage Debt – Calculate Your "Living Expenses"

Start by calculating all your "living expenses". Living expenses are the sum of all your monthly mandatory "fixed" expenses plus your "discretionary" spending. List all your living expenses by category and average each amount to calculate the total amount you spend each month..

Categorize your living expenses into 2 groups:

Fixed expenses- These expenses include rent / mortgage, car payments, utilities, minimum amount required to make loan / credit card payments, food, etc. Include everything that you must pay out every month. We'll need this to calculate your monthly "burn rate". In other words, how much cash you will have to spend every month on the necessities.

Discretionary or non-mandatory expenses: These expenses include dining out, entertainment, vacations, memberships, shopping for non-essentials, etc. Discretionary expenses are any purchases that are not absolutely necessary each month.

Think about which discretionary expenses can be cut. This is not easy because you'll need to give up some things that you enjoy. Keep it all in perspective. This is temporary and is only for financial survival during your transition period. The more you save, the more cash you'll have left in savings to weather the time it takes to find the right job. It takes much longer to save money than it does to spend it, so be smart about it.

Monitoring your day to day living expenses is challenging. Computer programs like Quicken or other similar software programs do an excellent job in tracking and budgeting. Some budgeting apps are free and there are other low-cost alternatives. They are well worth the cost to help you while in transition. A simple excel or numbers spreadsheet will also suffice.

Whatever tracking method you choose, do the math and monitor your spending. Know what your *"burn rate"* is and how much cash you will "burn" through over time. This knowledge is critical to surviving longer without a steady income. The most important calculation you need to make is to figure out how long it will take before you are completely out of cash. This will give you a potential deadline to beat and should motivate you to get out there and find that next job.

Step 2: Manage Debt with Your Credit Cards

Running up credit card debt while in transition is very easy to do and should be avoided as much as possible. While it's easy to say, "don't use your credit cards", the reality is that you may need to use them and carry an expensive, monthly balance.

Before you go into more credit card debt, research the market and locate cards with the lowest % rate. This will keep your minimum payments lower. Avoid store credit cards as their monthly interest rates are often significantly higher than Visa or MasterCard's. Both work just as well for the same purpose. Stay away from cards that require immediate monthly payoffs like American Express. This will help in the event you need to carry a balance. Whatever you do, <u>don't get a credit card just for the points</u>. This is not the time to build up spending points. What's worse is those points cards often come with yearly membership fees.

Step 3: Find Income Sources

Since "cash is king", there may be other sources of income from that can keep you afloat during your transition period. Here are some ideas for other potential financial sources:

At the time of a layoff:

- ☐ **Severance** - Are you eligible for any type severance from the layoff? If you are, using the burn rate calculation described earlier, factor in the impact of the severance.

- ☐ **Valuables** - Do you possess any valuables such as old gold or jewelry, coins, collector items, etc. that could be sold when you approach the end of your cash reserves? Calculate what you think these are worth and be realistic.

- ☐ **Stocks** - What about any stocks or stock options from previous employers which could be sold to create emergency cash? How much are these worth at today's current prices?

- ☐ **Insurance Policies** – Do you have any insurance policies that could be converted into cash if you sold them?

- ☐ **Deferred Compensation Plan** - Do you have an old deferred compensation plan?

- ☐ **HELOC** - If you own your own home, you may want to raise cash through a Home Equity Line of Credit *or HELOC*. HELOC's used to be called "second trust deeds". Check to see if already have an open line of credit on your home. If so, how much can you borrow on your LOC (Line of Credit)? HELOC's were designed for capital improvements on homes or other real estate. However, they are often used to purchase cars or other capital items which are not really part of the design of these loans because of the tax deduction. Keep in mind that while HELOCS may be a source of cash while in transition, they do add to the debt on your home and during an audit, the IRS may look with disfavor on improper usage of a HELOC account.

- ☐ **401K or IRA** - Do you have a 401K or IRA account that you can draw from? Keep in mind if you are under 59 ½, you will be subject to a 10% exercise penalty and ordinary income tax on "premature" distributions from these plans. There are also hardship reasons you can use to withdraw but check with a financial planner before doing so. Keep in mind it is possible to take distributions from retirement account, and then replace them within 60 days. In this case, there are no penalties and this is called the "60-day rule". Most financial planners don't recommend using retirement funds to live on. However, as a last resort, and without any other options, you should do what you must do to survive financially during transition.

Deducting Job Search Expenses

There are job related expenses which can add up, especially when little to no income is coming in. Fortunately, job search related expenses are deductible on your federal income tax return, but only if you itemize your deductions. (Specific job search deduction details can be found on-line at irs.gov and search for IRS publication 529.) Use schedule A (Form 1040 or Form. 1040NR) to deduct job search expenses along with your medical, dental, home mortgage interest payments and charitable deductions.

There are guidelines that must be followed to be able to take the deduction. Expenses related to a job search are considered as "miscellaneous" but are subject to a 2% "floor." In plain English, this means the total of your miscellaneous expenses including tax preparation fees, subscription services, P.O. Box etc. must be more than 2% of your adjusted gross income (AGI) before you can take any deductions.

Assuming your adjusted gross income from unemployment is $21,600, you would have to report combined miscellaneous expenses of more than $432.00 which is 2% of $21,600 before any of your expenses become deductible. Once you have reached this threshold for miscellaneous expenses, you can then begin to deduct any amount beyond the $432.00. For this example, let's assume your total expenses were $1,250 for the year. This calculates as $1,250.00 in expenses minus the 2% of $21,600 "floor" or $432.00 which equals a remainder of $818.00 in tax deductions. (These tax rates are subject to change and are only used as an example).

Another rule is that you can only deduct expenses used in a job search for your current occupation. If you are a school teacher and are searching for another teaching position, your expenses after the 2% AIG rule are deductible. However, if you decide to return to school to become a nurse, you cannot legally deduct your job search expenses. This current occupation rule also applies if you are searching for your very first job. Your first job is considered as searching for a job in a different occupation and is also not deductible.

Here are some examples of job search deductions:

- On-line job / resume posting services are deductible. For example, if you upgrade your LinkedIn account to a paid monthly subscription to locate job postings, it is deductible. Other types of paid job sites are also deductible. However, with the exception of subscribing to LinkedIn, I do not recommend paying for access to paid job related websites as the benefits are few.

- ❏ The cost of preparing and mailing copies of your resume to perspective employers is deductible. This includes paid assistance from an individual or a service to support you in writing your resume or designing your letterhead or graphics. Other deductions include the cost of resume paper, envelopes, printing, letterhead and postage fees.

- ❏ The cost of telephone related expenses, including any long-distance or overseas charges to potential employers. You must keep detailed records of who and when you called to support these charges.

- ❏ You may deduct travel expenses including meals and lodging when looking for a new job. This includes the cost of travel by airplane, train, bus or car between your home and the employer. However, if you are reimbursed by the employer or travel using frequent flyer miles or a similar program, you cannot deduct the expense. Travel and transportation expenses for job interviews must be outside of your current residency and primarily taken to look for a new job. You cannot deduct expenses that are extravagant or that are for personal purposes.

- ❏ In general, the IRS rules applied to job search are the same as those for business travel expenses. A portion of your home can be deducted as "office space" but is subject to the IRS rules. If you opt to take what is called the simplified deduction, the IRS will give you a deduction of $5 per square foot of your home that is used for business, up to a maximum of 300 square feet, or $1,500. However, if your home office area is over 300 square feet, you are not eligible to take the simplified method. If you sell your house, the office space used as a deduction may be subject to tax issues.

- ❐ You can deduct transportation to and from the airport, hotel expenses, lodging, tips, dry cleaning and laundry as well as meals, providing it is not reimbursed by the employer. Be sure to keep detailed records to substantiate your deductions.

- ❐ Fees personally paid to agencies, career coaches, outplacement etc. are deductible providing you are looking for a job, even if you are currently employed. However, if in a later year, your employer pays you back for the employment agency fees, you must include the amount you receive in your gross income up to the amount of your tax benefit in the earlier year. If your former employer directly paid an employment agency for your outplacement services, it is not deductible. More information on this subject can be found in the IRS publication 525.

Non-deductible job search expenses:

- ❐ While uniforms are a legal deduction for business use, you cannot deduct the purchase of an interview suit, a shave and a haircut or new shoes. Even though these are required to make you more presentable, they are considered personal items and are not deductible.

- ❐ According to the IRS, if there was a substantial time period between the end of your last job and the time you started your job search, you cannot deduct your job search expenses. This is one of those nebulous rules that is not defined but requires use of common sense. If you took a month to get your head on straight, it is probably not considered "substantial". However, if you take off several months to travel and unwind, it might be considered substantial.

Step 1: Develop Job Transition Strategy — Define Your Job Criteria

Chapter 4

DECIDING WHAT YOU WANT TO DO NEXT

Defining Your Job Criteria

Regardless of whether you are considering a career change or are currently unemployed, many candidates don't know what they want to do next. This is not unusual. In fact, it is quite common. Career change occurs for many reasons. You don't like the work you do and want to make a change, you feel you have been passed over for opportunities, you are bored, or maybe you are just ready for something more challenging or different. How do you determine what's next?

In this chapter, we will focus on the process of self-assessment; something that is necessary for developing your job search strategy. By defining your personal criteria, we can explore options, ideas and strategies for establishing where you want to go on your career path.

Decide on a Career Direction

To map your personal job search strategy, start by determining what job you are looking for. If you enjoy your work, you are probably going to be successful doing it. Make sure your ideal job is something you can be successful doing and is relative to your experience and skills.

If your last position was a financial analyst, don't expect to be hired as the CFO in your next role. Look for a position that you would ideally like to obtain that is equal to or slightly better than the one you previously had. Job transition is an opportunity to make career / life changes to find the right job that suites your personal interests.

It is far more difficult to obtain a higher-level position than you previously had during unemployment so keep your role in perspective. Don't lie or exaggerate what you did in your last position or give it more prestigious titles. Be realistic in your self-assessment and don't underestimate your abilities either.

Consider Your "Personal Values"

While you are searching for what's next, focus on <u>what you value in life</u> rather than focusing on <u>what you desire</u>. Personal values can mean things like "freedom". Some people are very comfortable working in a rigid environment where they are told when they can take vacation or time off while others need extreme flexibility to take off whenever they feel the need. Freedom can also mean creating your own schedule or not being tied to being in the office.

Another example of *personal values* is "risk taking". Some people love to work in an environment of total risk (sales commission only jobs, start-up companies, etc.) where consistent performance means everything. Others prefer job security as the most important personal value over everything else. However, most people fall somewhere between the two extremes.

Other *personal values* may rely on social interaction vs. working alone; doing something that provides meaningful impact or being able to change in the world. You may seek creative or learning environments, balance, mission driven focus, independence or even job status.

Don't consider money or wealth a personal value. It is usually tied to another personal value like status or security. Keep in mind that certain values may be more readily aligned with certain types of careers.

When you are unhappy in your current job, chances are your *"personal values"* are being violated. Identifying your personal values is one of the best indicators of what might be a more satisfying career path.

Most people seek fulfillment in their jobs and being able to relate them to your personal values will be more fulfilling. Certainly interests, skill sets, and types of industries are important in finding the right job, but knowing your personal values will enhance your self-awareness and help you choose the right career path.

If you could create the perfect job environment, what personal values would mean the most to you on a day to day basis? **Define your personal values by making a list of your top 5 and ask yourself if the type of career you are seeking aligns with them.**

Relocation Considerations

If you are considering relocation as part of your job search, then be serious about relocating. Don't interview out of town if you have no intention of taking the job. You are wasting your own time as well as the employers time and money.

Don't use relocating as a way to run away from everything and get a fresh start. While relocation could jump start your career, it isn't necessarily the best way to build up your bank account. There are significant expenses involved in moving and they should not be underestimated. While the salaries paid in larger metro areas are usually higher, so are the expenses and the increase in doesn't necessarily make up for the difference.

Large metropolitan cities like New York, San Francisco, Los Angeles and Chicago are high cost/rent areas where you will need to pay a lot more for housing when compared to the lower cost of living in a smaller city.

Before you pursue any job that requires relocation, research the salary range (e.g. salary.com, etc.) for similar positions in the area you are looking at. Research the cost of housing. For example, someone moving from Buffalo, NY to Orange County California is going to have a significant challenge in housing affordability. Doing the research will provide you with a much better idea of what it costs to live in the area and what kind of salary you would need to be able to live there.

Career Change Exercise

If you are not sure what job you would ideally like, the following tables will provide you with an exercise that focuses on areas of personal interest. Most candidates have interests in a number of different functions, occupations or activities. However, they are unsure of how to translate these interests into careers that are appealing. Part of your plan should be deciding on exactly *what you want to do next* and should factor in your "personal values".

In the following exercise, you will be presented with a variety of areas that may or may not interest you. This is referred to as an "Interest Inventory". Rank your interest level for each question with a score of 1 through 4 with 4 being the highest and 1 the lowest.

BUSINESS ATTRIBUTES	RANK 1 THROUGH 4
A. Do you like to manage projects?	
B. Do you like to sell things?	
C. Do you like to make things happen?	
D. Do you like to speak to groups?	
E. Do you like to be the leader?	
F. Do you like to persuade others?	
TOTAL SCORE - BUSINESS ATTRIBUTES	

ORGANIZATIONAL ATTRIBUTES	RANK 1 THROUGH 4
A. Do you prefer working with a chain of command?	
B. Do you feel a need to know what is coming next?	
C. Do you like things to be orderly?	
D. Are you more comfortable in stable situations?	
E. Do you prefer well defined tasks?	
F. Are you more comfortable with office procedures?	
TOTAL SCORE - ORGANIZATIONAL ATTRIBUTES	

THEORETICAL ATTRIBUTES	RANK 1 THROUGH 4
A. Do you like to solve puzzles?	
B. Do you enjoy math and science?	
C. Do you like ambiguous challenges?	
D. Do you like to read and study?	
E. Do you like to investigate physical things?	
F. Do you like to think through problems?	
TOTAL SCORE - THEORETICAL ATTRIBUTES	

ARTISTIC ATTRIBUTES	RANK 1 THROUGH 4
A. Are you more comfortable working alone?	
B. Do you prefer freedom over structure?	
C. Are you comfortable in unconventional solutions?	
D. Do you like to express yourself?	
E. Do you like aesthetic statements?	
F. Do you like to think through problems?	
TOTAL SCORE - ARTISTIC ATTRIBUTES	

MECHANICAL ATTRIBUTES	RANK 1 THROUGH 4
A. Do you like working with tools?	
B. Do you like to operate machinery?	
C. Do you like repairing things?	
D. Do you like physical work?	
E. Do you like to work outdoors?	
F. Do you like to work with your hands?	
TOTAL SCORE FOR MECHANICAL ATTRIBUTES	

SOCIAL ATTRIBUTES	RANK 1 THROUGH 4
A. Do you like to work with other people?	
B. Do you like to be part of a group or team?	
C. Do you like to train other people?	
D. Do you spend a lot of time social networking?	
E. Do you like to care for or help others?	
F. Do you like to supervise others?	
TOTAL SCORE FOR SOCIAL ATTRIBUTES	

RECORD THE TOTAL SCORE FOR EACH CATEGORY HERE	TOTAL SCORE
BUSINESS ATTRIBUTES	
ORGANIZATIONAL ATTRIBUTES	
THEORETICAL ATTRIBUTES	
ARTISTIC ATTRIBUTES	

	LIST YOUR **TOP 3** ATTRIBUTE SCORES IN THE TABLE BELOW:
#1	
#2	
#3	

Attributes as They Relate to Career Fields

Now that you have scores for each of the attribute categories listed, we will need to translate your interests into specific employment areas. The tables below show a relationship between the categories you scored highest and the types of positions related to those interest categories.

Using your **THREE HIGHEST ATTRIBUTE CATEGORIES** put an **X in the box** next to the job titles or career fields that you find most appealing in the following tables.

Once you have completed putting x's in each of the boxes, the next step is to list your skills and experience to see if they match the positions that best fit your attributes and areas of interest. In addition, consider how each type of job would relate to your personal values.

A	BUSINESS ATTRIBUTES	B	ORGANIZATIONAL ATTRIBUTES
	Business owner		Accountant / Auditor
	Buyer/ Merchandiser		Banking Professional
	Caterer		Bookkeeper / Financial Analyst
	Public Affairs Director		Credit Manager
	Food Service Manager		Court Reporter
	Hotel Manager		Dietician
	Human Resources Manager		Food Service Manager
	Inside Sales Representative		IRS Professional
	Manufacturer's Representative		Medical Assistant
	Marketing Specialist		Pharmacist
	Purchasing Agent		Teacher
	Real Estate Agent		Tradeshow Manger
	Sales Representative		Trainer
	Travel Agent		

C	THEORETICAL ATTRIBUTES	D	ARTISTIC ATTRIBUTES
	Actuary		Advertising
	Chemist		Architect
	Chiropractor		Art Teacher
	College Professor		Author / Writer
	Computer programmer		Broadcaster
	Dental Hygienist		Chef
	Electronic Technician		Computer Game Designer
	Geologist		Copy writer
	Medical Technician		Film / Video Editor
	Mathematician		Foreign Language Instructor
	Physical Therapist		Graphics Designer
	Science Instructor		Interior Decorator
	Physician		Librarian
	Surveyor		Photographer
	Systems Analyst		Public Relations Specialist
			Videographer
			Web Designer

E	MECHANICAL ATTRIBUTES	F	SOCIAL ATTRIBUTES
	Aircraft Technician		Athletic Trainer
	Auto Mechanic / Engineering		Child Care Worker
	Brick layer		Cosmetologist
	Carpenter		Customer Service Representative
	CAD Designer		Dental Hygienist
	Computer Technician		Elementary Teacher
	Customer Support		Guidance Counselor
	Electrician		News Reporter / Media
	Fabricator		Nurse
	Firefighter		Occupational Therapist
	Home Remodeling		Ministry
	Home Staging / Entertainment		Non-profit Director
	Manufacturing Engineer		Sales Representative
	Metal Worker		Social Worker
	Painter		Social Media Specialist
	Plumber		Special Education Teacher
	Police Officer		
	Prototype Design		
	Repairman (Equipment)		

	Telecommunications Specialist
	Tool & Die Maker
	Welder

Transferable Skills

Job skills <u>are transferable</u> so don't limit yourself to only jobs that you have done before. Look at the skill chart below and determine your last industry / occupation? Keep in mind that this is a general representation and your specific industry or skills may not be shown in the examples. What other industries / sectors are your skills transferable to?

Skill Chart

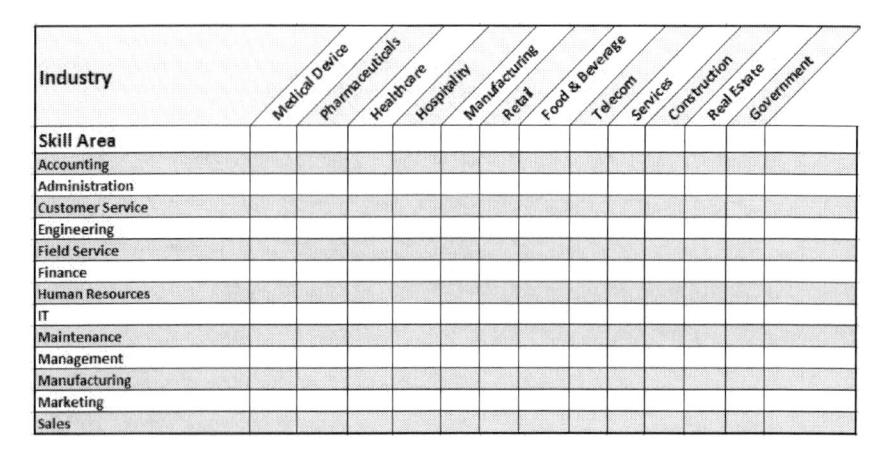

Industry	Medical Device	Pharmaceuticals	Healthcare	Hospitality	Manufacturing	Retail	Food & Beverage	Telecom	Services	Construction	Real Estate	Government
Skill Area												
Accounting												
Administration												
Customer Service												
Engineering												
Field Service												
Finance												
Human Resources												
IT												
Maintenance												
Management												
Manufacturing												
Marketing												
Sales												

Figure 4-1: Skill Chart

If your skills are in financial accounting, they can be applied to a variety of industries. If you came from the auto industry and are looking to apply for a position with a medical device company, don't be discouraged away from applying simply because the job description says, "must have medical device accounting". <u>Job descriptions are guidelines and are by no means the final</u>

word. Companies look for talent and will often accept related skills or experience. Here is an example of "related skills":

Peter's Story

Peter recently graduated from college and was seeking an *entry level sales position*. While attending one of my classes he asked me; "how can I possibly get a position in corporate sales when the job description requires a minimum of 3 years of sales experience? I have been a college student and don't have any sales experience."

I asked Peter if he had any prior work experience. He replied, "I currently work evenings and weekends as a waiter in an upscale restaurant. I started there in my freshman year and have been working there ever since".

I asked Peter to describe what he does in his role related to "selling" customers. He explained; "Well I take their drink order and ask if they would like to order appetizers. The more they order, the larger the bill, which gets me a bigger tip".

For nearly four years, Peter has been working at his job, learning to sell customers extra drinks, appetizers and desserts to increase his sales volume. This is a good example of *related* sales experience.

Peter also mentioned that he has customers that come in regularly and ask to sit in his section. Good customer service is also an important skill set that is related to being a good sales person.

Peter can use this know how to demonstrate to a potential employer that he has the relative sales experience needed for an entry level sales position. The point is, don't be discouraged by what is specified on a job description. Know your skills and focus on jobs that can use those skills.

Defining Your Job Search Criteria

To help you find the perfect career opportunity, you'll need to decide what criteria is most important to you. This will help you define where you would ideally like to work, how far you would like to commute, what skills you'll need, etc. This step is very important in setting a career path for your future.

Review each of the following to determine your search criteria:

- ☐ **What Size Company Do I Want to Work for? (Employees, Revenue $)**

    There are significant differences related to working in different size companies. Some people find it difficult to fit in large size organizations if they've worked in smaller ones and vice versa. Here are some general characteristics to consider:

    – *Large Corporation ($100M+)* – Company stability, more internal opportunities but more competition to advance. Structured environment, functional depth, specific area of job focus

    – *Mid Cap Company ($10M - $100M)* – Less stable than large companies, easier to stand out but fewer internal opportunities, etc. Wider job focus and functional responsibilities, less support functions, etc.

    – *Small / Start-up Company* – Least stable, requires multi-tasking, small community. High risk, high reward, perform many jobs. Before joining a startup company, be sure to evaluate your tolerance for risk and stability. Startups are ideal target companies if you are looking for equity / ownership as part of your search criteria.

- ☐ **Geographical Area – In what location do you want to work?**

    - Are you willing to relocate? If so, with what limitations?

- ☐ **How Far are You Willing to Commute?**

    - If you are not willing to relocate, are you willing to take a position that requires you to live away for the week or month or fly in and out?

    - How long are willing to commute? A 1 or 2-hour commute may not seem that difficult, but after you start the job, it may become tedious and may not be something you want to do long term.

- ☐ **Are You Willing to Travel as Part of the Job?**

    - Some positions require more travel than others. Consider the positive and negative aspects of traveling.

    - What percentage of time are you willing to travel?

    - Are you willing to be away from your family?

- ☐ **What Industry Do I Want to Work In?**

    – Do you prefer to stay in your current industry?

    - If not, what new industry would you like to work in?

    - Are your skills transferable?

- ☐ **Does Your New Career Path Require Additional Schooling?**

    - Do you need to return to school to obtain the skills and are you willing to?

    - Have you been considering finally getting that bachelor's or master's degree?

Keep in mind that, according to the U.S. Census Bureau, there is a million-dollar difference when comparing the lifetime earnings of someone with a high school diploma vs. a bachelor's degree. The earnings go up by another half million dollars if you add on a master's degree.

In today's online world, it's easier than ever to get a degree or certification. You can get a degree online in your spare time from an accredited university right from the comfort of your own home.

☐ **What Salary Do You Need to Sustain Your Lifestyle?**

- What is the minimum salary you'll need to cover your fixed expenses?
- What salary range should you be looking for?
- What other compensation might come with the position? (Equity, company car, cell phone, etc.)

☐ **What Job / Title are You Looking For?**

- Should I take a lower level job to get in a new industry?
- Should I try for a higher job level in my current industry?
- What is the amount of authority are you are looking for?

☐ **Are You or Would You Consider a New Industry?**

- From a market perspective, is your current / last industry experiencing a slow down?
- Are there job functions in your workplace that are no longer being utilized or are they being outsourced?
- Are you keeping up to date to know what's shaping your industry and the associated job market? By doing this you'll be better prepared to implement strategies to win a new job or launch yourself into an entirely new career.
- Research any new industry to before pursuing it.

☐ **Are You Considering Self Employment or Starting a Business?**

- While you are in transition, have you considered working for yourself?

- Are you self-disciplined enough to make effective decisions and manage multiple tasks?

Summarize Your Self-assessment and Job Criteria

I suggest you follow one of Bear Bryant's (US football coach 1913-1983) three rules of coaching which is "Have a plan for everything". Anyone who has ever been successful in business has started by assessing their business opportunities and defining what is needed to be successful.

The same applies to your personal job search. To develop a plan, create a written summary of your job criteria decisions and which marketing tools will be needed for your job search. We will call this your *"Job Search Plan"*.

The following is a template to provide a general guideline outlining the criteria to effectively plan your job search. Some of the terms and ideas may be new or unfamiliar so I will provide greater detail on how to develop them where needed.

JOB SEARCH PLAN

STATE THE TITLE OF THE POSITION THAT YOU ARE SEEKING

(Example) - Sales Manager, IT Manager, Administrative Assistant, etc. This is the time to start thinking through what position you are interested in, what your criteria is and make a decision. You can't go anywhere if you don't know where which direction your headed.

Include the reasons why you believe you are qualified to work in that type of position.

STATE YOUR TRANSFERABLE VALUE

What value do you offer a potential employer? List your top 3 - 5 accomplishments related to the functional position (job title) you are seeking. This will be part of your "personal brand" and will be covered in another chapter. Here is an example of the accomplishments someone might say they offer a potential employer:

- Promoted to sales manager in 2016
- Track record of sales management - increased sales; 2016 - 6%, 2017 - 7%, and 2018 - 9% year over year
- Qualifications include experience in the computer, wireless, and PC Board industries. Background includes extensive strategic and tactical experience in both Fortune 500 companies as well as Pre-IPO's. Professional training includes BS and MBA degrees from Cal State College with minor in engineering.

STATE YOUR PERSONAL GOALS

State your top 5 – 10 goals in order of preference in locating a position. Here is a brief sample of your plan's areas of focus:

- ❒ Search for a senior sales management position.
- ❒ Locate a position with a minimum salary of $_____K
- ❒ Land a position before (specify MONTH AND YEAR)
- ❒ Relocate to _____ or remain in _____ (where ever your current city is.

- ☐ Need flexibility in my schedule to be able to spend time with my family/children
- ☐ Prefer to work for a larger company ($100M+) for greater stability

CREATE A MARKETING TOOL SET

CHECK OFF AS YOU COMPLETE THE FOLLOWING DOCUMENTS: (We will cover how to create each of these in detail in upcoming chapters)

- ☐ Resume
- ☐ Complete LinkedIn Profile
- ☐ Biography or 1 Page Summary
- ☐ Cover Letter/message to employer
- ☐ Endorsements
- ☐ Post-Meeting Packet that you can leave behind after meeting with a potential employer

STATE THE LOCATION YOU WOULD LIKE TO WORK IN

State your desired location – what location are you are willing to relocate to?

- Remain local – no relocation OR
- New England area or NYC metro area OR
- Boston, Chicago or Miami OR
- London, Paris or Beijing

LIST YOUR IDEAL (TARGET) COMPANIES INCLUDING THOSE IN RELATED INDUSTRIES

List the industries and companies you would like to work at, specifically those that could utilize your skills. For example, if your experience is in *computer sales*, you might be targeting manufacturing companies such as Apple, HP, Dell, etc. A related industry to target would be PC Board Manufacturing, Disc drives, Power supplies, Printers, Computer accessories, etc.

Examples of RELATED Target companies:

- PC computer hardware – Apple, HP, Dell, etc.
- PC Board Manufacturing – Sanmina, Merit, TTM, etc.
- Disc Drive Manufacturing – Western Digital, Seagate, Samsung, etc.
- Printers – HP, Brother, Cannon, etc.

Create a table listing of 25-50 companies that you would like to work for. Research the names and titles of the managers that could potentially hire you. *(We will cover more details of how to use this in an upcoming chapter).* Include network contacts that know the manager or might provide an introduction.

Here is an example of what your table / spreadsheet section should look like:

COMPANY	INDUSTRY	TARGET PERSON	NETWORK CONTACT	PHONE #'s	COMMENTS
Dell	Computer Hardware	John Smith, VP Sales	Sally Douglas CFO	714-260-3398	Worked with Sally Douglas at HP
HP	Computer Hardware	John Youngman, VP Sales	Brian Wilson Dir of Finance	949-267-8793	My brother knows Brian Wilson through an Army contact
Western Digital	Disc Drives	Michael Harris, VP Sales and Marketing	Bob Narley Purchasing	949-237-2356	Found Bob Narley through a LinkedIn contact

TACTICAL PLAN (WHAT DO I NEED TO DO TO FIND OPPORTUNITES)

- ☐ **Networking** – Where can you go to meet other people that could help me (networking)? Organizations and Memberships, meeting participation, reaching out to others to find target contacts. *(We will cover networking in another chapter)*

- ☐ **Recruiters** – Reach out to recruiters if it fits your skill set. (LinkedIn, personal contacts) *(We will cover working with recruiters in another chapter)*

- ☐ **Search Tools** – Utilize search tools (locating key contacts in target companies, creating LinkedIn profile visibility, locating positions, Social media tools - LinkedIn Profile, Google Profile, Jibber Jobber etc.). *(We will cover details on LinkedIn and targeting companies in upcoming chapters)*

SELF-EMPLOYMENT - A Different Career Path

Another possible option to consider is self-employment. Let's face it. Some people have difficulty working for others and prefer to control their own destiny. I think it's important to consider as an option if you believe this is something you can personally handle and want to do.

If you are motivated and are considering becoming self-employed, you'll need to fully commit! You can be successful running your own business, you but it won't be easy at first. There are many advantages to becoming your own boss but transitioning from what you are familiar with a steady paycheck requires some advanced thinking and planning.

Before you run off and start the next Facebook or Wal-Mart, make sure you conduct a self-analysis to be decide if you have the right stuff to start your own business.

Ask yourself the following questions. If you answer "no" to any of the questions, you should shy away from self-employment or at least focus on learning how to change your behavior before you do. If you answer "yes", to all of them then self-employment may be for you. However, be sure to conduct more research on the viability of your business idea BEFORE acting. Answer the following questions:

- ❐ Are you prepared to take a risk, lose money or lower your current standard of living temporarily for the needs of the business? Keep in mind that most businesses don't make any money (operate at a loss) for the first few years so you need to be prepared for this.

- ☐ Do you have good credit or have family members that are willing to help finance your business temporarily?
- ☐ Are you willing to work 10 to 12 hours a day, possibly 7 days per week, at least in the beginning?
- ☐ Can you tolerate obstacles that will cause you delays or setbacks?
- ☐ Do you have the stamina to go the course while you figure out if your business idea is working?
- ☐ Can you develop a business plan to map out a step by step process to get your business going?
- ☐ Are you a well-organized multi-tasker?
- ☐ Are you a self-starter that initiates tasks to completion without instruction?
- ☐ Are you someone who can make fast and decisive decisions?
- ☐ Are you someone who is unafraid to reach out to others
- ☐ Do you get along with all types of people personalities?

Self-Employment – Be Ready to do It All

Being self-employed requires that you behave different. To prepare yourself and increase your chances of success, focus on adapting your thinking to focus on the small business world.

Business planning skills are a very important part of self-employment. Be sure to study and learn more about them before you take any risks or business start-up actions. If you are not familiar with writing a business plan or it seems overwhelming to create one, consider taking a business course, talk to other small business owners or seek out a small-business adviser.

Make sure you are comfortable with the technical business information you're getting involved with. Seek out others who run similar types of businesses you are thinking about. Prepare and ask plenty of questions. There are plenty of on-line resources on many different types of businesses.

Starting a business requires that you have the financial resources. <u>You should have at least one year's worth of income before you begin</u>. To improve your chances of survival, it is best not to have your entire income emanate from any one source. Within eight to nine months you'll know whether your business is sustainable. You cannot worry about job security because there isn't any. The entire business can collapse from a single event, but you need to be ok with taking that risk. Remember the reward on the other side is equally great.

At first, you might feel very isolated because there is little to no interaction with anyone. No ringing phones, formal meetings or planes to catch. This depends on the type of business you move in to and requires adjusting to a new environment.

You'll need to start creating the demand for your business. If you become a professional consultant, it doesn't mean clients will immediately knock on your door and pay $100+ an hour for your expertise. To get clients, you'll need to market yourself, advertise or become your own advertisement when you network. There are costs associated with marketing materials even if you only print business cards and build a website. No matter what you decide on, be professional. Very few clients will pay for something that looks amateur or shoddy.

How much do you charge? Do you charge by the hour, by the day or by the project? These are questions many professional consultants ask themselves. Calculate what you earned per hour as an employee plus the cost of insurance and other benefits. Don't forget overhead costs involved for rent, utilities, equipment, etc. which need to be part of your charges.

Keep in mind that you can expect to spend 10 to 20% of your time with administrative tasks which are usually not billable. These include writing proposals, billing clients, book keeping, and written correspondence. Charges vary by industry, but it is suggested to charge two to three times what you made in your W-2. A typical profit margin should be at minimum, 20 to 25%.

In professional consulting, make sure you have an agreement with the client in writing that defines the scope of work (SOW), billing rates including unforeseen expenses, liabilities and any other obligations. There are many on-line standard contracts available, but you will need to customize them for your specific application. It also helps to have an attorney look at it to make sure you define each party's obligations.

Self-employment can be both personally and financially rewarding but it comes at a risk and it's not for everyone. Think carefully through the details before you decide what's next.

Step 2: Create Your Marketing Tools

Define Your Value and Messaging

Chapter 5

DEVELOPING YOUR PERSONAL BRAND

After determining the position (job title) you are seeking and the type of companies you would like to work for, you'll need to be able to communicate the specific skills and expertise that you offer. In other words, be clear in describing the value you bring when speaking to a potential employer.

It's all about the value you can offer the employer

Whether you have decided to make a career change or have become unemployed, the starting point is typically updating a resume and LinkedIn profile. The correct starting point is actually defining your value BEFORE you begin to create or update your resume/LinkedIn profile.

You need to be able describe in detail the *value* you bring to a potential employer as it relates to their needs. Just having an updated resume will not help you stand out from the crowd unless you can say something that captures the employers' attention.

This is what is called your *"personal brand"*. Your *"personal brand"* is essentially the establishment of an image or impression in the mind of others about you.

Be original - Create your own brand

One of the classic mistakes candidates make is to use a resume or LinkedIn profile written by someone and modify with their own information. There is nothing wrong with copying someone else's format or layout. The problem is, the content isn't written about you. It is written about someone else! Modifying the descriptions in someone else's resume will not effectively convey your own strengths and value.

Think of it this way. If you had to create an advertisement, what would you say about the product? Would you simply want to fill it with text or would you focus on creating a message that grabs the reader's attention? The same thing applies to your resume and LinkedIn profile. You need to emphasize what sets you apart from the rest, not copy someone else's format and describe every job you ever had in specific detail.

Marketing You

When you are looking for a job, the product you are marketing is you! Like any product, there is a certain amount of inventory in the market at any one time. The more similar products there are in the market, the more competitive the market becomes.

Recruiters and placement agencies often refer to candidates as "inventory". They use their inventory to ensure they have pre-screened, qualified candidates available to respond immediately when asked to fill a position.

Leila's Story

Leila was a bright, young business development manager who was looking to make a career change. With several years of industry experience at the same company, Leila told me she was bored with her current job. Her goal was to locate a position where she could travel extensively, especially to China. When I asked what she was doing to locate a new position, she told me she was applying for jobs online, but getting no responses.

After reviewing her resume, I noted that it was not very well written and was poorly formatted. To a potential employer, a poorly written / formatted resume is a subliminal red flag that the candidate does not pay attention to detail.

I had to listen closely as Leila spoke with a strong Chinese accent. She told me that English was her second language and her native language was Mandarin Chinese. When I asked about her bilingual skills, she went on to explain that she was very fluent, both verbally and in written Chinese. She also had experience doing business with a number of Chinese companies.

She needed to learn that being bilingual was a very valuable skill, especially to companies doing extensive business in China. Her ability to communicate in Chinese was useful and was an important part of her "personal brand". However, it wasn't even mentioned on her resume!

We spent some time together restructuring the format of her resume to prominently display her fluency and experience in Chinese near the top. With her newly updated resume, she received multiple job offers within a few weeks! Today, Leila has the dream job she wanted, traveling regularly to China and the far east.

The Value Proposition

In the world of marketing and advertising, the messaging created to describe any products "value" is called a *"value proposition"*. In human capital and recruiting, this value proposition is referred to as your *"personal brand"*. Your personal brand should contain information about your *"specialized knowledge"* which is transferrable and most importantly, relevant to the employer.

Why is this value proposition so important? It's the description of what makes you valuable. An employer needs to be able to recognize your value quickly. A strong value proposition will <u>help you get noticed and land a position faster</u>. Companies that can quickly recognize how you would be useful in their organization will jump at the opportunity to scoop up such a valuable player.

A *value proposition* or *personal brand* speaks to the positioning of your skills and experience that distinctly defines the capabilities you offer in your industry and against other candidates (competing for the same job). The *"story"* you create about your value should be presented in such a way to make employers eager to consider the skills you offer. It is very important that your story positions you as unique and differentiates you from your peers.

Storytelling

To demonstrate the importance of good content, think of this simple analogy. Imagine you run a online publication. Your primary function is to provide interesting content for the reader. Each "story" you create must provide value to the reader.

Now imagine if the staff didn't invest much time writing good stories but spent most of their time making sure the magazine had nice graphics and had good formatting. Do you think the magazine would provide much if any "value" to its readers? The "story" is everything to the publication, just as your "story" (value proposition) is, to a potential employer.

Marketing process for the job seeker

To develop your *"personal brand"*, you'll need to follow the same 3 process steps used to market anything; (1) Create value, (2) Develop marketing materials and (3) Communicate the value. This marketing process is shown in the following graphic. The most important part of this process is the first step; creating value.

Marketing Process for the Job Seeker

Create Your Value For An Employer	Develop The Marketing Materials To Describe Your Value	Determine The Methods To Communicate Your Value
STEP 1	**STEP 2**	**STEP 3**
• Your Specialized Knowledge	• Your Resume	• Networking Contacts
• Your Accomplishments	• Your Cover Letters	• Meetings & Functions
• Your Industry Experience	• Your LinkedIn Profile	• LinkedIn Contacts
• Your Strengths & Expertise	• Your Post Interview Packet	• Google Profile / Searches
• Learning The Employers Needs	• Your Business Cards	• Your On-line Presence
	• Your References	

Figure 5-1: Marketing Process for the Job Seeker

In this chapter, we are going to focus on helping you determine what your personal "value" is. In subsequent chapters we will discuss the other 2 steps, showing how to use your value (personal brand) to develop your marketing materials and how to communicate them to potential employers.

During a job search, the emphasis is on skills and experience. You must know what your core skills are, how transferable they are to other jobs and how they relate to each position you apply for. If you want to move into a new function that requires new skills for a particular job, you'll need to recognize what those skills are.

To help you be the best "product" you are capable of, start by recognizing what your core skills are and what they can offer to a potential employer.

Consistent Messaging

Another fundamental rule of marketing is that you consistently communicate the same value proposition in all your marketing materials (Resume, LinkedIn profile, biography, business cards, post interview packet, social media, elevator statement, etc.).

Conveying your value should be succinct as well as consistent. Trying to describe everything you ever did in your life on your resume overloads the reader with too much information.

How to Create Your Personal Brand

In the world of marketing, advertising agencies are paid a lot of money for ideas or what is referred to as "ideation". Agencies carry a huge responsibility to create an image for a their clients and their brand(s). It is the agencies job to create the marketing campaigns to give each brand a perceived value.

Large corporations spend hundreds of millions of dollars with agencies on ad campaigns just to get you to remember their brand name. It's all about creating a brand that buyers know and will select because of the brands perceived value. As someone who spent the bulk of my career in marketing, here is how I define a brand:

A name becomes a brand when people are willing to pay more for it's products or services simply because the brands' name is on it.

This is exactly why you need a personal brand. You need to create an image that people are willing to pay for. Since you likely have little to no experience in the advertising world, we will walk through this process.

Determine what makes you valuable

To create your personal brand, <u>you will first need to determine what makes you valuable.</u> Start by listing your **core skills**. What are you good at and why should an employer consider you as a candidate? Keep in mind, there are different types of core skills you possess. Here are some examples:

- *Technical Skills* – *Writing computer code/ HTML, quality/manufacturing expertise, etc.*

- *Functional Skills* - *Marketing analysis, budgeting, business planning, etc.*

- *Personal Skills* – *Creative, innovative, organized, etc.*

Creating your personal brand

<u>Define your technical, functional and personal skills and make a list of what they are</u>. In addition, list of all your accomplishments throughout your business career. These accomplishments don't need to be earth shattering or major breakthroughs. They can simply be examples of things you are proud of. Let's define your core skills by answering the following questions:

- What are your technical, functional and personal skills?

- What are your career accomplishments? What have you been recognized for? (Awards, certificates, promotions, recognition letters, etc.)

- What specialized knowledge do you have?

- What is unique about you? (Skills, certifications, degrees, etc.)
- What areas or industries do have considerable experience in?
- What makes you different from other candidates?
- What positive things would others say about you?
- What are your strongest skills?

Making a SALE

In most cases, you are not the only candidate applying for a position. Your personal brand needs to differentiate you from the rest of the field. Try to evaluate yourself from different perspectives - your industry, your expertise and who the people are that you would compete against you for the position. When creating your "value" proposition, it should meet what I call the "SALE" criteria. SALE is my acronym for the following attributes:

Specialized knowledge – Unique specialized knowledge or expertise that you bring to an employer.

Accomplishments – Show what have you accomplished in your employment/schooling. Accomplishments demonstrate results.

Leverage core competencies – How will your skills/strengths match the company's core competencies?

Experience – Show that you have related or first-hand experience in the job function.

To help you develop your value proposition, meeting the "SALE" criteria, answer these questions:

1. What does the employer need or what is the problem that hiring you solves?

2. What unique specialized knowledge or expertise do you provide that solves that need or that problem?

3. How is your expertise or experience different or better than those offered by others that would compete for this same position?

4. How does your expertise fit or leverage the organizations strengths / core competencies?

5. What experience do you have relative to the job function that makes you unique?

How Do I Validate How I am Perceived?

Now that we've defined your technical, functional and personal skills, you need to know if others that know you, perceive you in the same way. While we all have personal perceptions of the skills we have and the value we bring, some are more realistic than others. It's important that you do a reality check to learn how people actually perceive your business skills.

The easiest way to learn this is to conduct some simple research with business colleagues, friends and family. Start by creating a small "accountability" network group. Ask members of your group to tell you what core skills they believe you have and what would make you valuable to an employer.

The best method is accomplish this is by using anonymous feedback. If members of your group cannot provide this type of feedback

anonymously, they may not be totally honest in order not to offend you. Get together with the group and ask them to write their true opinion on a secret ballot or create an anonymous survey using surveymonkey.com or other type of free survey service. If the feedback is not what you expected or they can't describe your skills, you'll need to work on improving how others perceive you.

Here is an example of the differences in the way you may perceive yourself versus how others perceive you:

YOUR OPINION OF YOU	HOW OTHERS PERCEIVE YOU
Great communicator	Doesn't say much – quiet person
Strong leadership skills	Follows the crowd
Financial expert	Others think you are in operations
Good organizational skills	Never organizes or manages meetings

Figure 5-2: How Others Perceive You

Conveying Your Value

The skills that make you unique and valuable are based on your expertise and experience, not where you worked or what you did in the job. Too often candidates specify what did in their job role, not what they accomplished. Employers aren't necessarily interested in where you worked. They care about the skills and experience you bring and if they fit the needs of their company.

Your transferable skills are what qualifies you as a viable candidate if you are making a career change. They can help you cross over from one occupation or industry to another, providing they fit the employers need.

Short and to the Point

In the advertising world, it is well understood that to convey value, you don't need to say much. Unless you are in marketing and already know this, it is quite common to say as much as possible to sell yourself. The problem is, saying too much often dilutes your value.

Let's assume you are an advertising agency tasked with creating an ad for new cars. How would you communicate the value of your client's vehicle brand in a 30 second commercial?

You don't have time to talk about the plush leather seats, the premium sound system, or to detail the car's performance. You only have 30 seconds in a commercial to say everything you can say! The automotive industry regularly works within these time constraints and spends millions to make us remember their brands.

So how do the experts do it? Let's look at one of the top automobile ad campaigns that has been running the same brand ad for years. BMW has created a simple, but brilliant value proposition in a statement that says; BMW the *"Ultimate Driving Machine"*. You probably wouldn't even know who they are if they used their full company name which is "Bavarian Motor Works". They spend millions advertising "BMW – the Ultimate Driving Machine" to make sure you remember it.

Based on perceptions, if you were asked; which large-size luxury brand would you rank first; BMW's 6-Series, given its reputation for quality and excellence, or Hyundai's Genesis G90 luxury sedan? Due to its extensive brand visibility, most people would select BMW. However, in a 2018 US World and News report ranking the best large-size luxury vehicles, Hyundai's Genesis ranked #2, far ahead of BMW's 6-Series which was only ranked #6.

BMW has done an excellent job at marketing the quality and performance of their automobiles in the mind of the consumer. The reality is despite this perception, the BMW 6-Series ranks behind 5 others in the US World and News report. In the same report, both Tesla Model S and the Genesis G90 luxury sedan ranked #1 and #2 respectively at the top of this category. In the world of marketing, perception is reality!

Using Accomplishments to Convey Value

One of the best ways to communicate your value as an employee is to state your value through *accomplishments*. For resumes, use a list of business related accomplishments you've created for yourself and state them wherever you can in *measurable results*. For example, explain what you have achieved in your work history, describing results that:

- Reduced costs
- Increased revenue or profit
- Saved an important customer
- Grew business
- Increased efficiency
- Improved quality
- Improved customer satisfaction
- Overcame competitors
- Improved employee satisfaction
- Opened new markets
- Implemented systems

- Solved a problem
- Created something new
- Provided effective training

To show an example, let's assume your skills are in the HEALTHCARE industry. Beside reducing COSTS, one of the primary areas of focus in healthcare today is about the QUALITY of care. Some accomplishments may be described quantitatively while others may be described qualitatively. Here are examples of how HEALTHCARE industry accomplishments can be listed as bullet points:

- Improved quality of patient outcomes by 8% through development of innovative new critical care blood delivery system.

- Reduced disease incidence by 3% and improved overall health of patient base by implementing new scrub procedure.

- Expanded health care services, programs, and outreach to meet patient needs, while increasing overall hospital revenue by 11%

- Attained 99% compliance level and maintained stringent regulatory requirements providing a positive impact on quality of care

- Implemented advanced health care and health care support technologies to reduce cost and shorten patient stays

Communicating Your Value

When you are presented with an opportunity to communicate your value during a conversation, the last thing you want to do is ramble on about how great you are. Just like the BMW TV commercial, you need to be able to speak a 60 second verbal commercial about you!

When someone asks the question "what do you do"; your response should be brief and memorable. It should articulate who you are and what makes you unique. Deliver your value in a short, succinct statement. You can further expand your value using example analogies and stories to make it come alive.

- Who are you?
- What is unique about you?
- How do you generate success?

Understanding Levels of Communication

How much information you can convey to someone depends on time constraints. For example, attending a meeting presents more time than a casual hello at a networking event. The illustration below demonstrates how much can be communicated based on the amount of time your situation presents.

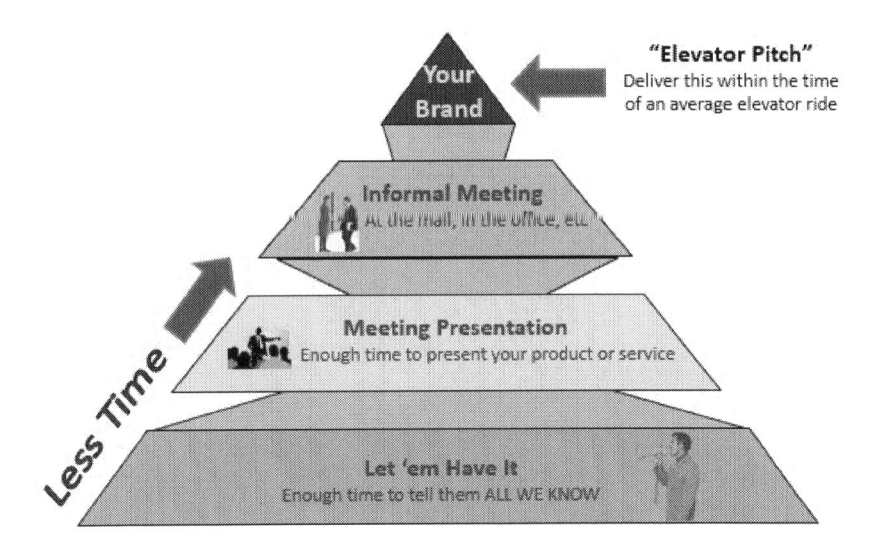

Figure 5-3: Levels of Communication

When meeting with a potential employer, you want to impress them with your knowledge and skills. Unfortunately, the most common practice is to attempt to communicate as much as possible to self-promote.

Too often I've seen candidates "let 'em have it", saying everything they could possibly say about themselves. This creates an awkward situation where the listener really doesn't want to hear you go on and on about how great you are. Think "billboard" not "bulletin board"!

In other situations, you may have an opportunity to formally present yourself during the introductory portion of a presentation. Other times you may opportunistically meet someone in the hallway for a chat. You need to be able to adjust your personal brand pitch and deliver it within the time constraints presented.

Communicating your personal brand in a limited timeframe requires that you are able to summarize the key points about you. To be effective, you need to condense your statement into something that is very short and to the point. This will allow you to effectively communicate your value to people in one on one situations.

The Elevator "Pitch"

The concept of the "elevator pitch" was originally developed as part of a sales course. This scenario concept was created to describe selling to a client in a very short window of time.

The scenario is; you meet an important potential customer in an elevator. The challenge is, you only have enough time for the elevator to travel from the bottom floor to the top floor. Your elevator pitch needs to <u>create enough interest for the client to get them to agree to a future meeting</u>.

The point of the elevator speech analogy was to create interest, <u>not to make a sale during the elevator ride</u>! For the job seeker, you too should be able to communicate your own *"verbal commercial"* or *"elevator speech"* within the same amount of time it takes to ride up an elevator from the bottom floor to the top!

When meeting with a potential employer or someone of influence, you want to generate enough interest to get them to agree on a future meeting or obtain an interview. The important lesson here is to learn that the goal of the elevator pitch is not to land a job on the spot, but to get the listener interested enough to want to learn more about you.

Your "elevator pitch" (verbal commercial) answers the question "So what do you do"? It should define your profession, value and describe what makes you unique or special. Your elevator pitch can be a simple statement and should not be more than 2 or 3 sentences maximum. It should contain your skill, expertise or competency. It should articulate your value and the impact you could potentially make as part of the company.

Elements of an Elevator Pitch

So what makes a great elevator pitch? To create your memorable elevator statement, the content should contain each of the following elements:

1. Position / Job Title - Mention the title of the position you are seeking. No one can help you if they don't know what type of position you are looking for.

2. Industry - State the industry you are targeting. It is usually based on your experience in that industry and it tells the listener what industry you're focused on.

3. Proof Point or Strength - Tell the listener why you are qualified / unique / have certain strengths. Everyone says they are great so you really need to validate your statement with some form of proof. Here is an example:

*"I am a **quality manager** in **aerospace / defense manufacturing** with a **six-sigma black belt certification**".*

From this statement, the listener can derive that the **position** you are seeking is a **quality manager,** the **industry** you are targeting is **aerospace / defense.** They also hear that you are in **manufacturing** and your **proof point** is your attainment of a **six-sigma black belt.**

Note: If you don't know what a six-sigma black belt is, Six Sigma is a set of techniques and tools for process improvement which were

developed by Motorola in 1986 and adapted by General Electric. A black belt signifies the level of expertise in the methodology of Total Quality Management (TQM) referring to the Motorola six sigma principles.

While your personal proof point may not be as strong as someone who has a six-sigma background, you can use statements that are self-promoting based on your track record. Here are a few examples of this with the keywords emphasized:

"I am a **Marketing Communications manager** in the **auto industry** with **over 5 years' experience**. I **help businesses build and promote lasting brands**."

"I am a **Sales Rep** in **the medical device industry** with over 4 years' experience. I have **a solid track record, winning top product line sales awards 2 out of 4 years**."

If the listener latches on to something you said, be prepared to articulate the details of your accomplishment or expertise.

Keep it Short

When I listen to people deliver their elevator pitch, about 75 – 80% go on and on while conveying little to no value. The reason; they are too focused on what they did, not what they accomplished. Rambling on for several minutes is far too long to provide information.

If you had to trim your positioning statement down to only 60 - 90 seconds, what would you leave out? Instead of babbling on about your life story, why not cut right to the chase. What do you offer the employer?

Describe a proof point or strength that you offer an employer; *"I help inside sales teams turn phone prospects into sales orders"* This tells the listener exactly what you do.

Telling them that you are a "motivated, results oriented, hardworking individual etc., etc." is not something of interest. Everyone pretty much says the very same thing! Focus on what you offer and have accomplished, not about your work ethic.

Professional Delivery

The other important piece to developing an effective elevator statement s delivery. Listening to someone who looks at the floor, stumbling over words, trying to remember the exact way the statement was rehearsed weakens the listeners' perception of you.

The more you try to cram in, the greater the chance this will happen. Focus on the short, meaningful information that describes what we previously discussed. This short statement is the reason I sometimes refer to this as an *elevator statement* rather than an *elevator pitch*.

This elevator statement is very important as is utilized when speaking to people at networking group events. The same applies with anyone so they understand what you do and what you are looking for. Your statement should be personal, well-rehearsed and memorable. Again, it should not be your life story or a long drawn out soap box speech.

Be yourself, look directly at your audience and deliver it with believability. Once you become comfortable with saying it, you can augment it with an additional sentence or two keeping it at a minute or less.

When you deliver your elevator statement as an introduction, it should sound something like; *"Good Morning! I'm Samantha Manville. I have 4 years' experience as a manger in the tele-sales industry. I help inside sales teams turn phone prospects into sales orders".*

Keep it simple, speak slowly, and focus on what you offer. Practice this as practice makes perfect!

Communicating Accomplishments

To demonstrate how powerful marketing can be, brands using creative marketing have proven to be very successful in convincing consumers to pay outrageously high prices for products which are essentially made at market cost.

I doubt the cost of manufacturing a Rolex watch is <u>10 times</u> what a top end Seiko watch costs to make. Yet, the Rolex brand commands an incredible mark up in price.

What Rolex has accomplished through their marketing is to fashion an image in the consumers' mind that **<u>wearing a Rolex is a status symbol of wealth and success</u>**. It also projects an image that a Rolex watch keeps flawless, precise time. Just as Rolex uses creative marketing to create value, you need to be able to communicate the value of your core skills and accomplishments to potential employers in the same manner.

PAR Statements

When it comes to conveying value during a discussion or job interview, my preferred method is to articulate personal accomplishments using what are known as **"PAR" (Problem-Action-Result) statements**. These are also referred to as **Challenge–Action–Benefit statements**. PAR statements provide a short, step by step methodology to tell a story.

Keep your statements relevant to the potential employer and position when applying or interviewing. PAR statements should not be more than 1 or 2 paragraphs or a 1-minute discussion. Categorize them by the type of accomplishment (e.g. customer service related, etc.) and the skills and expertise you used to solve the problem.

Here is a breakdown of what information is needed for each of the 3 parts of PAR statement:

PROBLEM-ACTION-RESULT (PAR) STATEMENTS

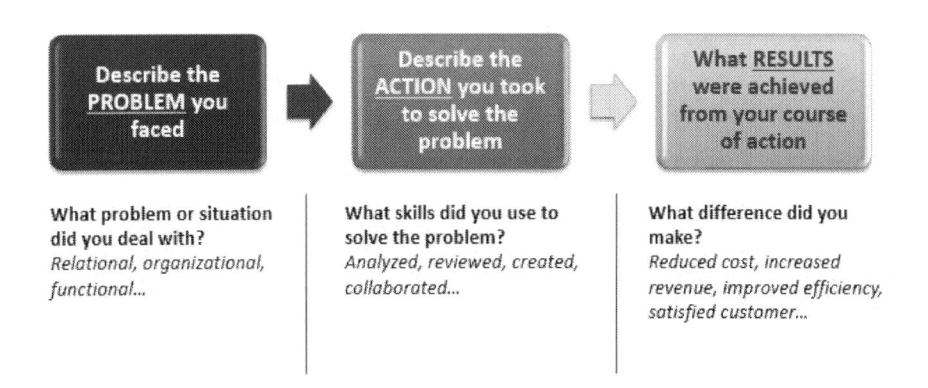

Describe the **PROBLEM** you faced	Describe the **ACTION** you took to solve the problem	What **RESULTS** were achieved from your course of action
What problem or situation did you deal with? *Relational, organizational, functional...*	What skills did you use to solve the problem? *Analyzed, reviewed, created, collaborated...*	What difference did you make? *Reduced cost, increased revenue, improved efficiency, satisfied customer...*

Figure 5-4: PAR Statements

PROBLEM: Describe the business problem or situation you dealt with. Be specific but brief in describing the problem. Was it a problem with people, process, or product related?

ACTION: Describe the action you took to correct the problem. How did you expect to solve it? What skills or resources did you use? Discuss the process you used in your action

RESULT: What were the results? How much of an impact did your actions make in terms of cost, efficiency, quality, time, customer satisfaction, etc.?

Power Stories

By using your PAR statements as a complete, combined response describing the *problem, action and results*, you create what I refer to as a *"power* story". The *power story* demonstrates your "strength" and experience in tackling a similar problem or situation.

Here are some sample PAR statements expressed as *"power stories"*:

PAR Statement (Power Story) Sample I

"After joining Bogus Company as Director of Marketing, I observed that my department was slow in getting new products developed and out into the market. I restructured the marketing team into an upstream and downstream organization. This new structure shortened the time to develop a new product by 4 months over previous product development cycles".

Here is how that "Power Story" breaks down as a PAR statement:

PROBLEM: Slow product development time to market

ACTION: Reorganized the department into upstream and downstream marketing

RESULT: Shortened the time to develop a new product by 4 months – Implying an increase in the number of new products developed over a period

PAR Statement (Power Story) Sample II

"As the Inside Sales Manager at XYZ company, I managed a CRM implementation project system that resulted in a 10% increase in productivity and sales growth of 7% year over year."

PROBLEM: The Company was not effectively tracking sales and you were given the task to implement a new CRM system and make it work.

ACTION: Managed successful implementation of the project

RESULT: Increased productivity by 10% and sales growth by 7% year over year.

Exit Statement

Accomplishments are one thing, but we cannot ignore the fact that you could be unemployed while you are seeking a new position. Not only is it important to communicate your value, but you also need to explain why you are not currently working and why you are looking for job.

The reason you are no longer in your most recent job is called an *"exit statement"*. An exit statement should be brief and positive. Any form of negative response can easily sink your chances of getting the job during an interview.

Create your exit statement and be prepared to deliver it spontaneously whenever needed. Here some sample exit statements:

"After working at X company for the last 3 years, I decided to look for an opportunity that was a better match for my skills and interests. I gave my notice so I could spend my full time locating that opportunity."

"My company recently consolidated two divisions into one. As a result, many positions were eliminated including my own."

"Due to a downturn in business, the HR organization had to eliminate several positions to align with the company's financial goals and my position was part of that reduction."

In many cases a simple, brief explanation will move you past this obstacle during a discussion or in an interview.

Step 2

Create Your Marketing Tools → Create Your Self-Marketing Tools

Chapter 6

CREATE YOUR SELF-MARKETING TOOLS

Now that you've defined what core skills you have and what makes you valuable as a *brand*, the next step is to develop the marketing tools to communicate your personal brand to potential employers.

Since marketing is such an important part of the job search process, I've focused the next several chapters of this book to help you create the types of marketing materials you'll need to *shorten your job search*. While we will cover these in far greater details in upcoming chapters, here is a quick overview of the key marketing tools you'll need for success:

- ❒ **Job Search Plan** – I provided a template for this back in Chapter 4. Elements of your job search plan should include self-assessment and career vision, including search objectives. Once you have developed your "value proposition", you'll need to plug your strengths into the job search plan template.

☐ **Resume or CV** – A resume is the standard format used by employers to review your qualifications and accomplishments. *Always keep in mind that the objective of a resume is to get you an interview,* so it needs to read as a good match to the job description. To help you develop yours, I have devoted the next chapter to creating a winning resume.

☐ **One Page Summary or Biography** – A one-page Summary is sometimes referred to as a *Biography*. It is a concise summary of your professional and/or personal background which conveys the VALUE you bring to a potential employer. Your one-page *summary document* should contain your transferable skills (Specialized accounting, Oracle expertise, etc.), conveying accomplishments using the PAR method (Problem-Action-Result) and using metrics wherever possible. It should also include the personal attributes that define your strengths; leadership, creativity, problem solving, etc. It is a free form document which means you can format it anyway you choose. Keep in mind that this type of document is designed for a hiring manager to read. It is not one to send to human resources who prefer traditional resumes. We'll explore how to use a one-page summary in greater detail in the next chapter on resumes.

☐ **LinkedIn Profile** - LinkedIn has become as important as a resume. It is the most useful on-line form of job search, utilizing social media. LinkedIn is a powerful business tool for both recruiters and employers who are searching for candidates. Maintaining a social media presence is key to getting a potential employer or recruiter to find you. Since LinkedIn is such an important tool, we will cover using it to search for people, companies, and jobs in much greater detail in Chapter 9 - *Using LinkedIn In Your Job Search*.

- **Cover Letters** – While cover letters are becoming less and less important with on line applications and ATS systems, there are some situations where using cover letters are just as important as a reading a resume or 1-page summary. In general, recruiters don't even read cover letters anymore. However, hiring managers, especially those in smaller companies as well as those companies that don't have ATS systems, typically do read cover letters. The reason; they are small and still sort and file resumes manually. For those that read cover letters, the average employer spends 15 seconds or less looking at your information. If your cover letter convinces the hiring manager that your résumé is worth a look, you have a better chance of getting to the "Yes" pile. The best cover letters explain your value through select details from your résumé and expand upon them. They offer a method to succinctly explain how your core skills and experience can benefit the prospective employer.

- **Post-Interview / Meeting Packet / Personal Marketing Portfolio** – How will an employer remember you after looking at several candidates? How can you differentiate yourself from the rest of the pack? Here again, standard classic marketing techniques can be used. When a salesperson meets with a customer, they often leave behind a brochure or packet of information for the client. The information describes what they offer, why it is different from the competition, and how it will benefit them. The same marketing applies for employment candidates. The post-interview / meeting packet is a collection of materials about you. They may consist of samples of career accomplishments or work, awards or certifications, articles, patents, or a host of other copies of selected items. You may also choose to use this material in a *Personal Marketing Portfolio* to verify what you say about your value in an interview or meeting.

- ☐ **Networking** – Because networking is such an important function in the job search process, I have devoted chapter 11 to this subject. Statistics show that a significant majority of all professional positions are found through networking, not job postings. When you network with others, you gain valuable insights about yourself, gather information about opportunities, and connect with people. By meeting regularly, when people get to know you, they may even recommend you for a position.

- ☐ **Business Cards** – The primary purpose of a business card is to hand out during networking meetings. Your business card should be memorable and not like everyone else's. When you are unique, people will remember you so get creative!

- ☐ **Targeting Companies** – Instead of sending resumes into cyberspace chasing job postings, the *Targeting Companies* methodology is a far more effective method to increase the probability of success. It is important to understand how to utilize the many search resources and tools to identify and target companies. Since the Targeting Companies methodology is such an effective way to find jobs, we will cover it in much greater detail in Chapter 10 - *Targeting Companies*.

Step 2: Create Your Marketing Tools — Writing A Winning Resume

Chapter 7

HOW TO WRITE A WINNING RESUME

Before we go into the details of what makes a winning resume (the one that gets chosen), let's be clear on the goal of your resume:

A resume is <u>NOT to tell your life story</u>; the goal of a resume is to get past an employer's screening process and get you to an interview!

Even if an employer found you on LinkedIn or you located a job and applied online, the resume is still a very important job search tool and is the most accepted form of communication with employers. Somewhere in the process, the employer will most likely ask you to submit a resume. For this reason, we will focus this chapter on the details of what makes a winning resume.

Over the years, resume use has been driven by a need to standardize an information format that can help a screener quickly recognize if an applicant matches the qualifications of a position. While the resume has become a standard format for listing qualifications, experience, and education, it also provides an easy method for potential employers to reject candidates.

Why is it easy to reject candidates? Because a typical resume is really nothing more than a list of where you worked. If it doesn't match the experience the employer is looking for, it's easy to reject. However, there are things you can do to make your resume more appealing and lessen its chance of rejection.

How Much Time Is Spent Reviewing Resumes?

According to surveys, your resume has about 15 seconds or less to capture an employer's attention! Some hiring managers say a typical screener spends only 8-15 seconds on the initial review. The truth is, the majority of resumes are never read beyond the first page!

If a resume passes this first look, they may spend an additional 30 seconds to give it a "yes" or "no" to move along in the process. Just knowing this will help you structure your resume so that it does a better job appealing to the potential employer or recruiter.

To create a winning resume, the most important aspect is that it resembles the job you're applying for. *It is very important to tailor your resume for every position you apply for.* Look for key words and the requested qualifications in job postings. Modify your resume as you need to using the same key words and phrases. Remember, there is no such thing as a universal resume!

Resume Length - Number of Pages

As a rule, your resume should not be longer than two pages. Why do we suggest limiting the resume to two pages? Simply because <u>no one will read it!</u> Candidates often ramble on about irrelevant or redundant experiences, creating multiple pages of wasted space. I've seen this often with IT professionals who attempt to list every piece of hardware and every software system they have ever worked with.

There are always exceptions, but you'll want your resume to be a neat, one or two-page document. The notion that a resume should only be one page is nonsense. Someone who is older and experienced may require 2 ½ pages to cover their accomplishments and work history. This guideline was likely created to prevent candidates from telling their entire life story on a long resume.

Longer resumes only work if your resume is interesting and well written. When you have a long resume that says everything possible about you, it will probably not keep the reader's attention. It doesn't mean that you're not a good candidate; it says that you're not focused. As mentioned earlier, there is no rule as to the length of a resume. What it communicates is what's important.

Some people believe that resumes shouldn't be longer than one page. They end up trying to squeeze their experiences onto one page and end up deleting some of their more impressive achievements. Whatever you write, think about each sentence and focus it on the same objective; "Will this statement help me get an interview?"

Resume Layout / Styles

There are several resume styles and layouts to consider, depending on the length of your employment experience, skills, expertise and education. Deciding which one is best for you is a matter of the position applied for, geography and personal choice.

While there may be more, there are generally 4 different layout / styles of resumes that we will cover later in this chapter and will provide examples. These are chronological resumes, functional resumes, achievement resumes and targeted resumes. Chronological resumes are by far the most common. More on this later in this chapter.

Curriculum Vitae (CV)

If you are applying for a position in academics or employment in Europe, the Middle East, Africa, or Asia, you may be asked to send your Curriculum Vitae instead of your resume. A *Curriculum Vitae*, more commonly referred to by its shorthand abbreviation CV (a Latin term meaning course of life), is a format that is more detailed and extensive than a resume.

Unlike the resume, which lists your work history and experiences, along with your skills and education, the CV is a far more comprehensive document. It goes beyond a simple mention of education and work experience and often provides details of your achievements, awards, honors, and publications.

The CV format is commonly used internationally, specifically in the U.K., Ireland, and New Zealand. It is also used at universities when they are looking to hire teaching staff. The CV is so common in mainland Europe that there is even a European Union CV format available for download on the web. This can be quite helpful if you are applying to work abroad. Unlike a resume, which is typically one or two pages, a CV can be three, six, or a dozen pages all depending on your details and professional achievements.

Should you create a CV? If you are considering working abroad, it can be helpful to list extensive details of your career and education just in case you need to make one. At least you'll have a current list of all the things you've ever accomplished, a.k.a., a master document to pull from as you look for details to apply to specific positions. However, you don't need to create one right now unless you are applying abroad.

In this book, we will not be covering CV formats. Instead we will focus in detail on the most common resume formats. There are a number of elements in the structure of all resumes so we will start there.

Focus on the Top Portion of Your Resume

The style and layout of your resume is important, especially if it only gets a 15 second look. Since most screeners reading resumes don't look beyond the first 1/3 or 1/2 of the first page, make sure your resume shows your value right in the beginning.

Use Bullets, Not Paragraphs

Stay away from writing long paragraphs. Employers may either stop reading or just skip these long paragraphs all together. This is exactly what you *don't* want them to do with your resume.

You're much better off using white space and bullets effectively. Keep in mind that you can have too much of a good thing so be selective on how you will use formatting techniques. **Again, think like you are advertising on billboard, not a bulletin board!**

Starting At The Top

Time to create your winning resume! Start by listing your name on the very top of the resume. **Your Name** should be written in **Bold Font** using **16-point** font size. As a general guideline, using different font styles and text sizes; italics, underlining, etc. can often be more distractive then helpful.

Throughout your resume, stay with standard font formats such as **Arial or Times Roman**. If you use exotic, non-standard fonts, the screener may not have these fonts installed on their computer. As a result, the screeners' computer will substitute a default font, making your resume appear unformatted and sloppy.

Listing Your Contact Information

Next add your *phone number* and *email address* at the top under your name. Don't use an email address that a potential employer might find immature, offensive or unusual like *hotmama@gmail.com* or *ladiesman@yahoo.com*. While you may think these are funny or cute, a potential employer may not.

Harry F. O'Keefe
Cell:(617) 555-5555 • e-mail: hokeefe@gmail.com

There is no need to list your home address on your resume unless you live close to the employer. *The employer will get it from you when you come in to fill out paperwork.* Candidates have been eliminated without further consideration simply because an employer felt their address showed they lived too far away, presenting difficulty getting to work in bad weather or traffic.

Job Titles

You may want to consider listing a job title on your resume. This makes things easier for the employer as they don't have to wonder which job you're interested in or which hiring manager your resume should get forwarded to. The title should also be included if you used a cover letter but you want to be sure that both documents state it in case the two should get separated.

Summary Statements

Some believe that creating a *"summary"* at the top of the resume is your opportunity to provide the reader a brief but meaningful brief overview of the value you can provide to the employer.

For every job you apply for, move key information around making the first thing they see the most relevant to what they are looking for. If the position requires someone who is bi-lingual speaking English and Spanish, place that skill at or near the beginning of your resume (providing you do fluently speak both languages). Employers read from the beginning and may never get to the end. By placing the requested skills first, you will be more appealing as a candidate.

A good *summary statement* details three to five key strengths, experiences and interests that you can offer an employer. This title can also be listed as a header on the resume as; *Strengths, Skills, or Highlights*. Here is an example:

SUMMARY

Highly skilled copy editor with four years publishing experience. Expertise in social media and web design technology. Strong communication and organizational skills.

Another version of this could be to use a *"Summary of Qualifications"* which includes 3 to 6 bullet sentences as an overview of your background;

SUMMARY OF QUALIFICATIONS

"A results-oriented marketing communications professional. Strong communication and media skills. Demonstrated ability to create..." (Strong action phrases).

After you create your summary statement, ask yourself; does the summary make you stand out? At a glance, will the employer recognize that you are the one person that can do the job?

Objective Statements

For an entry-level position, use an *objective statement* on your resume instead of a summary statement. The *objective statement* is a clear, brief statement which outlines the type of employment you are seeking along with the title and or type of industry. It may also include the name of the company that you are applying to for personalization.

For someone with extensive experience, using an objective statement may convey the wrong message. As an example, having an objective statement: **"Seeking a challenging marketing position"** may be misinterpreted. If the position is you are seeking is a marketing communications manager position, this statement sends a subliminal message "I am looking for any type of marketing position including entry level".

Unlike the *summary statement* which provides what you offer the perspective employer, a well written objective statement provides a clear, brief statement outlining the type of employment you are seeking along with the title and or type of industry.

Too often, candidates lose their reader at the very beginning with a generic, overused type of statement. As an example, opening with an objective statement like the following is too general a statement and wastes the most valuable space on the resume:

Objective: Seeking a challenging position which enables me to utilize my skills and expertise in finance while offering me an opportunity for growth and advancement

If you chose to use an objective statement, it should be simple, well written and designed to convey your purpose and direction to a prospective employer. The statement spells out the specific position and what you are looking for. Here is an example of an entry level objective statement:

Job Objective: Desire a copy editing position with growth opportunities in a PR marketing firm.

If you use a summary statement or job objective, make sure you highlight your area of focus. However, if the information in your resume doesn't focus on any specific profession or industry, you may come off as a sporadic professional without any areas of expertise. Again, focus on making sure that you include relevant information that pertains to the job for which you are applying.

Resume Formatting and Font Sizes

As you progress through creating your resume, make it easy to read and keep formatting to a minimum. Ideally use an 11 or 12-point font size (never use a font smaller than 10 pt.). Pay careful attention to font size and space consistency. Use adequate white space between points and don't cram sentences. A clean, to the point resume will get much more attention than one crammed with loads of information.

Candidates cram far too much information into a resume by using smaller fonts. No one is going to read the microscopic detail so make your resume visually appealing on paper.

Font Sizing guidelines:

- **Your Name (Bold Font) – Use > 16-point size**
- **Headings (Bold Font) – Use > 14-point size**
- **Body text (Not Bold Font) – Use 11 or 12 point but no less than 10 point**
- **Margins (Use of White Space) - not less than 1 inch left & right sides, not less than 1 inch for the top and not less than 1 inch from the bottom**

Resume Job Titles

Keep your job titles generic. If your company had a special title for your position, e.g. "Neely Region Manager", use the generic Regional Sales Manager on your resume.

Resume Work Dates

For work date formats, don't use too much detail. It's not important to show the work dates in months unless your recently out of school and don't have much in the way of work experience. I suggest using the year only: (2013 – 2019 instead of 6/2013 – 5/2019). Exclude any employment history more than 10 – 12 years ago as these positions are usually no longer relevant to an employer.

Resume Education Details

When listing your education, unless you're someone who is right out of school, your degree should not be the first thing people see on your resume. Work experience trumps degrees. If you've been in the workforce more than four or five years, focus on your accomplishments. List your degrees, certificates and awards at the bottom of your resume.

If you're fresh out of school or have limited experience, it's acceptable to list your GPA along with your degrees. Here is something else to consider. Some recruiters don't recommend mentioning your GPA if it was less than a 3.7 and do not include GMAT scores below 650 if you're targeting a top firm.

Make sure to mention specific courses that are relevant to your job search along with any awards or scholarships you've earned. Any special training you've completed should also be included, so long as it's pertinent to the job you are applying for. For example, mentioning the military training and experience you've had may not be relevant for a finance job, but do mention it if you applied for a defense manufacturer.

List any work or community service jobs you have done while attending school. They may be relevant work experience. For example, law students who interned at law firms have relevant experience. Watching day to day activities and learning the interworking's of a law firm has value. Especially when a firm is looking to hire candidates fresh out of law school.

Resume Interests / Hobbies

Candidates often include their interests at the bottom of their resume, but these should only be provided if they demonstrate character or are relative to the job. For example, a software programmer applying for a developer position at a company that designs video games would want to list their favorite video games or levels of play they have reached.

Don't list unrelated skills, especially something that might spook a potential employer. I remember a very qualified candidate who submitted a resume listing his interests as:

"Kung-Fu master, Expert with knives and swords".

Even though the candidate was well qualified for the position, the hiring manager felt the candidate sounded like he could be a potentially *"violent"* person or someone who was focused on fighting. This was highly unlikely, but in the mind of the hiring manager, there was a potential risk and the candidate was immediately rejected.

Focus Your Resume on Accomplishments

The number one thing that will differentiate you from others on your resume is your prior work experience descriptions. The most common mistake candidates make is to list all the specific tasks and responsibilities you provided in your role, thinking the employer will know exactly what you're capable of.

The truth is employers generally don't care about what specific tasks you did, they are really interested in *what you accomplished in your previous roles and if can you do the same for them*. Without accomplishments, nothing truly sets you apart from other candidates.

In a recent survey of employers, **emphasizing results** was ranked the #1 item of importance for a resume. It is your accomplishments that will get the attention, not a job description of what you did. To highlight your accomplishments, list 3-5 key accomplishments that are relevant to the specific position you are applying for.

As a best practice, use bulleted accomplishments in your resume to highlight skills and achievements that relate to the employer's needs. Use a bullet point format with 1-2 sentences (not more than 4 sentences) each and modify your accomplishments to match the job requirements. The most important accomplishments should not be buried under each job; they should be at the very top of page 1 where the screener will see them. Make sure the bulleted accomplishments are in the relevant order that the screener will see them.

It is also important to list your accomplishments using descriptions that are more expressive. For example, saying *"worked as a web designer"* is far less impressive than saying you *"designed cutting edge and modern websites"*.

Use Action Verbs

As you create your resume, use action verbs for your accomplishments and show measurable results - savings ($), improvement (%), time gained or saved, etc. Make sure you don't use the same action verb for each bullet.

When designing the content, start each sentence with a descriptive action verb to add impact to your descriptions. Here is an extensive list of descriptive action verbs to utilize as a resource in writing your resume:

Accelerated   Accepted   Accomplished

Accrued
Achieved
Acted
Activated
Adapted
Added
Addressed
Adjusted
Administered
Advanced
Advertised
Advised
Advocated
Aided
Allocated
Analyzed
Answered
Applied
Appraised
Approved
Arbitrated
Arranged
Ascertained
Assembled
Assessed
Assigned
Assisted
Attained
Augmented
Audited
Authorized
Averted
Avoided
Awarded

Balanced
Bargained
Began
Bolstered
Boosted
Bought
Briefed
Brought

Budgeted
Built
Calculated
Captured
Cataloged
Centralized
Certified
Chaired
Changed
Charted
Checked
Clarified
Classified
Coached
Collaborated
Collected
Combined
Communicated
Compared
Compiled
Completed
Composed
Computed
Conceived
Conceptualized
Concluded
Condensed
Conducted
Conferred
Conserved
Consolidated
Constructed
Consulted
Consummated
Contacted
Continued
Contributed
Controlled
Converted
Conveyed
Convinced
Coordinated
Corrected

Corresponded
Counseled
Created
Critiqued
Cultivated
Customized

Decentralized
Debugged
Decided
Decreased
Defined
Delegated
Delivered
Demonstrated
Designated
Designed
Detected
Determined
Developed
Devised
Diagnosed
Directed
Discovered
Dispensed
Displayed
Dissected
Distributed
Diverted
Divided
Documented
Drafted

Earned
Edited
Educated
Effected
Elevated
Eliminated
Emphasized
Employed
Encouraged
Enforced

Engineered
Enhanced
Enlarged
Enlisted
Ensured
Entertained
Established
Estimated
Evaluated
Evolved
Examined
Executed
Expanded
Expedited
Experimented
Explained
Explored
Expressed
Extended
Extracted
Fabricated
Facilitated
Fashioned
Figured
Finalized
Fixed
Floated
Focused
Forecasted
Formed
Formulated
Fostered
Found
Framed
Fulfilled
Furnished

Gave
Gained
Gathered
Generated
Governed
Grossed

Guided

Halted
Handled
Headed
Heightened
Helped
Hired
Honed
Hosted
Hypothesized

Identified
Illustrated
Imagined
Implemented
Improved
Improvised
Incorporated
Increased
Indexed
Influenced
Informed
Initiated
Innovated
Inspected
Inspired
Installed
Integrated
Interacted
Interpreted
Interviewed
Instituted
Instructed
Insured
Interceded
Introduced
Invented
Inventoried
Investigated
Involved
Issued

Joined
Judged
Justified

Kept

Launched
Learned
Lectured
Led
Lifted
Liquidated
Listened
Located
Logged

Maintained
Managed
Manipulated
Marketed
Maximized
Measured
Mediated
Merged
Minimized
Mobilized
Modernized
Modified
Monitored
Motivated
Navigated
Negotiated
Netted

Observed
Obtained
Offered
Opened
Operated
Ordered
Orchestrated
Organized
Originated

Outlined
Overcame
Overhauled
Oversaw

Packaged
Passed
Participated
Penetrated
Performed
Persuaded
Photographed
Pinpointed
Piloted
Pioneered
Placed
Planned
Played
Predicted
Prepared
Prescribed
Presented
Presided
Prevented
Printed
Prioritized
Processed
Procured
Produced
Programmed
Projected
Promoted
Proofread
Proposed
Protected
Proved
Provided
Published
Publicized
Purchased

Qualified
Questioned

Raised
Ran
Rated
Reached
Realized
Reasoned
Received
Recommended
Reconciled
Recorded
Recruited
Redesigned
Reduced
Referred
Regulated
Rehabilitated
Rejected
Related
Remodeled
Rendered
Renegotiated
Reorganized
Repaired
Replaced
Reported
Represented
Researched
Reshaped
Resolved
Responded
Restored
Retrieved
Reversed
Reviewed
Revised
Revitalized
Routed

Saved
Scheduled
Screened
Searched

Secured
Selected
Separated
Served
Settled
Shaped
Shared
Signified
Simplified
Simulated
Sketched
Sold
Solved
Sorted
Sparked
Spearheaded
Specialized
Specified
Spoke
Sponsored
Staffed
Standardized
Started
Stated
Stimulated
Stipulated
Streamlined
Stretched
Strengthened
Structured
Studied
Succeeded
Suggested
Summarized
Supervised
Supplied
Supported
Surpassed
Surveyed
Sustained
Synthesized
Systematized
Tabulated

Targeted
Taught
Terminated
Tested
Tightened
Totaled
Traced
Tracked
Traded
Trained
Transcribed
Transferred
Transformed
Transmitted
Translated
Traveled
Trimmed
Tutored

Uncovered
Undertook
Unified
United
Updated
Upgraded
Used
Utilized

Validated
Varied
Verbalized
Verified
Vitalized
Volunteered

Weighed
Widened
Won
Worked
Wrote

Use PAR Statements - *Problem, Action, Result* to Communicate Accomplishments

As we discussed back in chapter 5, you can set yourself apart using PAR statements. Instead of writing what your responsibilities were for each job listed on the resume, focus on what you accomplished in each position.

List your accomplishments using PAR statements. Describe what you *accomplished in each job* in a bulleted format stating the *PROBLEM you faced*, *the ACTION you took and the RESULT that you achieved*. Build your resume with PAR statements instead of describing *what tasks you did in each job*.

To give it validity, provide how it was measured. Start with an action verb, followed by what you accomplished and then how you would measure it. State the information in terms of what was achieved.

For example, provide the details of what you increased or decreased, what you did to improve operations, increase revenues, strengthen bottom-line profits, reduce operating costs, enhance business processes, upgrade technologies, etc. Reinforce them with numbers whenever possible. Use percentages, dollar amounts or anything that will quantify how great each achievement was.

Focus on what is important to a company; money earned, or time saved. It'll make a huge difference in the eye of the employer. Here are some examples:

Example 1 – Vendor Training – Let's assume in a previous role, you were responsible for managing vendor training. As part of that responsibility, one of your key accomplishments was implementing a computer learning center. Instead of saying, *Responsible for the computer learning center* on your resume, create a PAR statement bullet point using the following elements:

- **Problem:** Reduce the cost of outside vendor training
- **Action:** "Implemented a computer learning center
- **Result**: "Reduced outside vendor training cost by $45K during the first year."

Compare the following two example descriptions for the same job. The first is *listed as a job by responsibility*. The second lists the same job as a *PAR statement*. Which of these do you think would have greater impact on a resume?

1. Describing the job by responsibility:
   "Responsible for the computer learning center"
   OR
2. Describing the job as PAR Statement:
   "Reduced the cost of outside vendor training by $45K through implementation of a computer learning center"

The addition of the $45K cost reduction makes the statement more powerful. Decreasing costs $45K anticipates the reviewer's question about whether you accomplished anything when you were responsible for the computer learning center. Whether $45K is a big expense or not, explaining how you did this adds credibility and provides insight into your strengths.

Example 2 – Customer Service Contracts - Let's assume as part of your customer service contract responsibilities, you instituted a customer call back program which proved to be successful in increasing the number of customer renewals. Instead of saying, *"Responsible for customer service contracts"* on your resume, create a PAR statement using the following elements:

- Problem: Need to increase customer service contract renewals
- Action: "Instituted a customer call back program."
- Result: "…resulting in a 22% increase in customer service contract renewals"

This is what the PAR statement might look like formatted on a resume:

Customer Service Manager   2015 - 2019
Bayside Industries, Andover, MA

- Increased customer service contract renewals by instituting a customer call back program which resulted in a 22% increase in renewals

You'll notice that each PAR statement example shows a *measurable* result. Focus on what is important to a company; results - money earned or saved, etc. It'll make a huge difference in the eye of the employer because it was measurable.

Use Expressive Descriptions

Let's assume you worked in the customer service department for over 3 years working in software telephone support. You may not have had the metrics that your manager had making this difficult to measure. However, through end of conversation phone surveys, you were ranked the highest customer service rep and received an award. How would you list this on your resume?

Candidates typically list what they did, describing each job by responsibility, rather than describing it by an accomplishment. Here is another example of a how a job description might typically be written on a resume:

- *Worked in customer service department providing telephone support. Answered calls and provided software support.*

Here is the same job listed as an accomplishment:

- *"Awarded "#1 Customer Service Rep" by providing outstanding customer software support services as ranked by client surveys."*

As shown in this and the previous examples, it's easy to distinguish which of these would be more appealing to a potential employer. Again, employers are not interested in what you did as much as what you accomplished. Your track record shows what you can do for them.

Professional Skills Listed as Accomplishments

The examples below lack specifics but could be used as a guideline for highlighting accomplishment areas on your resume: There are not enough pages to cover all the possible professional roles. In the following select examples, I have included a number of different professional skill sets in alphabetical order.

Administrative / Office Management

- List your accomplishments related to office organization and efficiency
- List your accomplishments related to your internal and external communications responsibilities

- List your accomplishments related to the introduction of technologies, systems or processes that your designed / implemented and their impact

- List your accomplishments related to improvements in efficiency, cost reduction or employee morale

- List your accomplishments related to training and development of other employees and the impact

College Graduate

- List an academic achievement (high school, college, university, post-secondary certification, or beyond) where your test scores or other achievements led to awards or scholarships.

- List an accomplishment where you worked in summer job or internship. Explain what you did and how it assisted the business in a supporting role and what kind of impact did it accomplish.

- List an accomplishment where you managed a budget or led an organization which led to a positive result. List how it was measured.

- List an accomplishment where you worked in a community or social organization which benefited others through your efforts. Explain what you did and how many people it helped.

CEO / Company President / General Manager

- List specific measurable increases in company performance - revenues, profits, EBITDA, or other financial accomplishments.

- List improvements in managing organizational infrastructure, productivity, performance yield, etc.

- List examples of leadership in developing strategic plans, long and short-term strategies for new business development

- List examples of recruiting top leadership teams and how they contributed to the success of the company

- List examples of leading mergers, acquisitions, joint ventures, and business-building initiatives

- List successful expansion into new markets, geographies, and how you obtained competitive market share

Computer / Information Technology

- List accomplishments related to your involvement in the design / implementation of new IT systems (SaS, Financial, etc.)

- List accomplishments related to your involvement in e-commerce, e-learning, web development, telecommunications, or other new technologies

- List accomplishments related to your successes with systems migration, conversion, integration, and implementation

- List accomplishments related to the financial benefits of technology implementation/ changes (e.g., revenue gains, cost reductions, productivity improvements)

- List accomplishments related to your development of new apps or software. Explain how this created new markets, disrupted the marketplace and financially impacted the company.

Consulting Professional

- List an accomplishment where you were responsible for reducing costs with outside vendors as well as managing outsourced third-party logistics providers. Achieved X% logistics cost savings by reducing returns, excess and obsolete inventory and implementing targeted outsourcing.
- List an accomplishment where you developed the annual company business plan based on a market research project you managed. Plan stated commitments for volumes, model mix, wholesale revenue, and selling expenses which resulted in a 9% increase in year over year revenue.
- List an accomplishment where you managed development of a new software platform to reduce costs with X company for post-delivery support allowing the company to utilize an online auction system for multiple vendors resulting a X% ($X) reduction in costs.

Customer Service / Support

- List an accomplishment where you corrected a problem resulting in retaining a key customer and saving the company from losing an account worth $X (how much?)
- List an accomplishment where you reduced customer service operating or overhead costs
- List an accomplishment where you improved customer service / customer satisfaction scores and by how much List an accomplishment where you improved industry rankings for quality of customer service organization and by how much

- List an accomplishment where you introduced or used automated customer service technologies and tools and show how much it saved / improved productivity, etc.

Engineering / Research and Development

- List accomplishments in engineering / design of new products and the associated financial impact on the organization or company.

- List accomplishments related to a redesign of existing products and their resulting financial, market, and customer impact.

- List accomplishments related to implementation of new engineering or design processes and their related positive financial impact.

- List design patents awarded and/or pending or implementation of new technologies to expedite engineering and expand capabilities.

- List accomplishments in project scheduling, engineering team management, staffing, leadership, etc.

Financial / Accounting

- List an accomplishment where you successfully negotiated a contract including dollar amounts, profits, cost savings, etc.

- List an accomplishment where you assisted /increased / improved revenue, profits, ROI, EBITDA, or other financial measurements and by how much

- List an accomplishment where you implemented a technology, an automated program, a tool, etc. to optimize business performance and what was the impact

- List an accomplishment where you were involved in a merger, acquisition, joint venture, or divestiture and its positive impact.

- List an accomplishment where you designed or implemented cost controls and provide the quantifiable results

- List an accomplishment where you worked with investors, pension plan administrators, board of directors, auditors, etc. and state the successful financial outcome

Human Resources

- List accomplishments related to your successes in locating, recruiting and hiring key employees and their impact on the organization

- List your accomplishments related to the introduction of employee policies, benefits and incentives and the effect on the morale

- List your accomplishments related to changes and improvements or cost reductions to employee benefits and their impact

- List your accomplishments related to employee training and development programs and their impact

- List your accomplishments related to the introduction or updating of HR information technology systems and its impact

Lawyer or Law Student

- List an accomplishment where you assisted in discovery including drafting deposition questions, interrogatories and requests for production of documents. Explain how it affected the final outcome.

- List an accomplishment where you convinced a jury to award $X in damages for your client and explain what you did to influence the jury.

- List an accomplishment where you prepared settlement agreement to resolve $X (type of contract) case between two parties.

- List an accomplishment where you researched issues pertaining to a pending motion which led to a dismissal in complex civil litigation case.

- List an accomplishment where you obtained a sentence reduction for a client in a criminal case from X years to X days in jail.

Marketing or Marketing Management

- List an accomplishment where you managed a social media campaign / advertising campaign which increased revenues by how much, reduced ad costs, generated an ROI of how much in $ or new customers.

- List a marketing accomplishment where you led a cross-functional team to develop and implement global advertising strategy for $X million in a specific targeted market. From your action, explain how it resulted in an X point increase in brand recognition and contributing to an X% year-over-year sales improvement (in $X Millions).

- List an accomplishment where you studied your key competitors branding strategies and analyzed their discount and pricing strategies as compared to your own. From this information, explain how your analysis made your company's products more competitive and how much it increased revenue.

- List marketing accomplishments focused on improved ROI, defining markets to increase revenues and improving process

- List an accomplishment where you managed a tradeshow, increased sales leads by how much, reduced the show cost by how much, generated an ROI of how much

- List an accomplishment as a product manager, where you introduced new products or services and state the results in revenues gained, reduced time to market, cost reductions, etc.

Operations / Manufacturing / Production

- List accomplishments related to how you managed / increased production / output, worker productivity, improved manufacturing turns, etc.

- List accomplishments related to how you reduced operating costs / overhead expenses

- List accomplishments related to how you implemented new technologies, processes, systems, and equipment which positively impacted productivity

- List accomplishments related to improvements in quality performance specifically those that resulted in quality certifications and awards

- List accomplishments related to your involvement in the design, set-up, and start-up of a new manufacturing facility and / or production lines

Sales or Sales Management / Business Development

- List an accomplishment where you won a key sale in your territory, how it captured a key client and how much revenue it generated / increased sales

- List the sales honors and awards you've won and list the percentages over quota when you did

- List an accomplishment where you developed a new territory or new market and show how much it increased

- List accomplishments where you increased revenues, profits, and market share and by how much

- List accomplishments focused on winning sales, clients and increasing revenues

- For sales managers, list an accomplishment where managed a sales team, what you did to grow the territory and provide the overall growth results over what period.

Veteran Transitioning to the Civilian Sector

- List an accomplishment that you responsible for in your duties - worked as a trauma medicine instructor for deploying units. Trained over X # of soldiers resulting in increased combat readiness.

- List a leadership accomplishment – As a non-commissioned officer, led a comprehensive redesign of the T-11 training program for X# airborne soldiers, reducing the number of training injuries by X%.

- List a work-related accomplishment that can transition to a civilian industry – worked as a helicopter mechanic, ensuring that all aircraft were flight worthy. Implemented a maintenance tracking system which reduced aircraft down time by X%.

The accomplishments listed here are just a sampling of the various functional areas within an organization. There are many industry-specific accomplishments that could be created relative to a specific position, industry or profession (e.g. teachers, stock brokers, retailers, etc.).

If examples of your job function are not listed, research how others identify and describe achievements in your specific industry or profession. Once you've listed all the accomplishments you've ever done in every company you have worked for, you'll be able to communicate your own accomplishments in your marketing. These accomplishments will be used again and again in your resume, bio, and other marketing materials.

Only Use Truthful and Accurate Information

Don't be tempted to exaggerate your skills or job titles. According to surveys, 50% of candidates said they do exaggerate on their resume. Exaggerated information is often a red flag for employers to check on the facts.

Statements like; *"Grew the territory sales from $100K to over $5M in 2 years"* is a sure-fire method to get the employer to question the statement's accuracy let alone focus suspicion about your personal integrity. If the employer even suspects you are lying, you will not get the job. If it is a true statement, you will need to explain the exact details of how you accomplished this stellar achievement.

With the heightened state of security in today's world, employers often hire companies who specialize in background checks for potential candidates. The higher the level of the position is, the greater the scrutiny.

Fake college degrees, exaggerated job titles and bogus descriptions are sure ways to reject you after a reference or background check. Worse yet after you're caught lying, you'll get fired! It will be increasing more difficult to deal with the stigma of being let go for fraud when you apply for your next position. Be as realistic and positive as possible about your experience without misstating or exaggerating the truth.

Resume Formats - Which Format is Right for You?

Now that we know how to state accomplishments, you'll need to choose the resume format that best fits your needs. There are several resume style types to consider. Each conveys information in a different manner in the order your accomplishments, experience and education are listed.

While there may be more, there are 4 general styles of resumes that we will cover;

- *Chronological resumes*
- *Functional resumes*
- *Achievement resumes*
- *Targeted resumes*

Chronological Resume

The chronological resume format is the most commonly used type. It gets its name from its format, where work experience is listed in a chronological order, starting with the most recent position first. Employers are very familiar with this format and usually prefer this layout. A chronological resume may or may not contain a summary. In any case, it should use bulleted points to highlight key skills, expertise and accomplishments.

While this is the most common format, there are flaws associated with the use of the chronological resume format. Listing dates and job descriptions can be counterproductive as it doesn't highlight what you are capable of. It only lists the places and dates where you've worked.

Too often, candidates try to cram everything they ever did into the chronological resume format. Providing too much information will not communicate what you are good at It will only overload the reviewer and reduce your chances to succeed as a candidate. Keep it simple, highlighting your accomplishments and describe them in bullet points, not paragraphs. Use action verbs and quantifying achievements whenever possible.

Education should also be provided with or without degrees. If you do not have a college degree, list your high school diploma and relevant training / certificates.

The chronological resume may also contain Professional Associations & Affiliations (or Community Involvement) if you can list organizations that are relevant to the position or can demonstrate leadership ability.

The following is a general example of how a ***chronological*** resume is formatted:

First and Last Name

(XXX) XXX-XXX • Yourname@email.com

SUMMARY: Include summary here

WORK EXPERIENCE:

Job Title (Most current)   **Dates**

Employer, City, State

- List your responsibilities, accomplishments, and skills

Job Title (Previous job)   **Dates**

Employer, City, State

- List your responsibilities, accomplishments, and skills

Job Title (Before previous)   **Dates**

Employer, City, State

- List your responsibilities, accomplishments, and skills

EDUCATION:

LICENSES AND CERTIFICATIONS:

AWARDS:

PROFESSIONAL MEMBERSHIPS:

Functional Resume

The functional resume gets its name from the way information is listed. It's format organizes your skills and accomplishments into job task (functional) groupings that support your job objective or summary .

The functional resume format allows you to list your strong points right at the top of the resume, either as a summary or as a list of accomplishments. It also provides the format to list your strengths by functional area (e.g. marketing, operations, finance, etc.) and place them closer to the top of the resume.

As you should do with any resume, be sure to modify the headings and resume information, based on the job you are applying for. Make it match what the employer needs.

A functional resume works well if you have a history of job hopping. Organizing the work experience by function draws attention to emphasizing *what* you have done instead of *where* you have done it.

The functional resume style also highlights your transferrable skills when you are looking to change occupations or industries. This format provides greater flexibility in presenting skills gained through personal experience or through low-paying or unpaid jobs.

It is useful for entry-level or reentry employees whose employment history is brief or scattered. As the chronological resume did, the functional resume should also contain education and professional affiliations.

Here is an example of a what a ***functional*** resume might look like:

HOW TO SHORTEN YOUR JOB SEARCH

Harry F. O'Keefe

Cell:(617) 555-5555 • e-mail: hokeefe@gmail.com

SUMMARY

Extensive experience in key account development, solution selling, and thorough knowledge of numerous sectors in the healthcare field, ranging from clinics and hospitals to drug manufacturers. My functional experience and knowledge is in sales and marketing as well as integration of these areas into account development and revenue growth.

MARKETING

- Designed national marketing program for Value Added Reseller (VAR) accounts, which generated over $19.5 million in sales and 11% year over year.
- Pioneered, printed and mailed a newsletter that successfully re-introduced the company's existing services and new services to over 15,000 potential clients with an 8% response rate.
- Researched, analyzed and implemented a database/image repository at Transamerica, Inc. Using the new system, managed and tracked over 1500 forms, resulting in reducing obsolescence by 21%.

SALES MANAGEMENT

- Instrumental in achieving the "Outstanding Performance Club" award for the office and many internal accolades for generating over $ 7.5M in sales vs. a $4M target quota in 2018.
- Created a Target Account program that closed a three-year, $ 2.5M contract with Apria Healthcare, the first new major account in two years.
- Directed and coordinated six sales representatives in using innovative ideas and cross-selling the full product mix which generated $1.35M in additional sales the first 15 months.

PROFESSIONAL EXPERIENCE

Minuteman Press – Northeast Sales & Marketing Manager 2008 - 2019

Stratacom - Account Executive   2004 - 2008

GARY CALVANESO

Standard Register Co. - Asst. Regional Sales Manager   2001 - 2004

EDUCATION

BS, Business Administration. Major in Marketing, Boston University College

Achievement /Accomplishment Resume

An achievement resume is exactly what the name implies. It combines both the chronological and functional resume formats while focusing on achievements. An achievement resume is designed to highlight what you accomplished during your career and should be relevant to the position you are applying for. If you are applying for a sales position and your accomplishments are in HR, they are may not be relevant.

Starting with a summary of your strengths and key skill sets, the accomplishments are listed in the upper portion of the first page. List key achievements that are relevant to the specific position you are applying for. Again, modify your accomplishments to match the job opening using the PAR format = Problem, Action, Result.

Like the chronological format, work experience is listed in chronological order with the most recent position first. Education is also listed. If you do not have a college degree, list your high school diploma and relevant training / certificates.

The achievement resume may also contain Professional Associations & Affiliations (or Community Involvement). Only list them if the organizations are relevant to the position or can demonstrate leadership ability. Here is an example of an *achievement* resume:

Cindy Manfield

Cell:(714) 522-1234 • e-mail: cindy.manfield@gmail.com

QUALIFICATIONS

Process Engineering Professional with proven success innovating new processes which revolutionize business practices.

- Developed and implemented cross-functional systems which resulted in an 80% increase in the multi-customer manufacturing process at *Jazz Semiconductor, Inc.*
- Increased order processing 30% by analyzing, defining, and documenting an optimal customer order procedure

CAREER ACCOMPLISHMENTS

- At Jazz Semiconductor, reduced manufacturing process cycle time 20% and increased repeatability 50% through the creation of a project management database and 2 new effective and efficient manufacturing processes.
- Designed process documentation framework for the entire organization which resulted in ISO 9001 compliance certification.
- Reduced internal software customizations by 90% through identification and elimination of unnecessary software functionalities, resulting in a $150,000 per year cost reduction for external technical support costs.

PROFESSIONAL EXPERIENCE

JAZZ SEMICONDUCTOR, INC., 2009 - Present

Quality Systems Engineer

- Reinvigorated stalled project teams by surveying team members to determine the size and scope of issues, identifying root cause problems, and redeploying resources.
- Reduced process documentation time 30% by developing metrics and implementing reporting systems.
- Created and led training on problem solving, process documentation, database usage, and root cause analysis for all levels of the organization, including executive management.

EDUCATION

- **CALIFORNIA STATE POLYTECHNIC UNIVERSITY**, Pomona, California - *Bachelor of Science in Industrial Engineering, Minor in Total Quality Management*

PROFESSIONAL AFFILIATIONS

- American Society of Quality Section 0701: Vice Chair, 2011-Present; Programs Committee, 2006-Present; Secretary, 2008-2010; Member 2006-Present.

Targeted Resume or One Pager

The targeted resume / "one pager" is somewhat different than other the others mentioned as it has a different intended purpose. A targeted resume should not be used as a general format to send to human resources when applying for a position. This format is designed to be a quick glance, one-page document that is ideal for sharing directly with the hiring manager. It focuses on the skills you bring, rather than when and where you worked.

The targeted resume focuses on a obtaining a specific position or job target. It presents your capabilities and accomplishments that support this type of position, eliminating all unrelated data. As you review the format, you'll notice it does not list specific work dates, but rather years of experience. Specific dates for places you've worked aren't important other than to show gaps in employment and length of time spent in each role.

This resume starts with a well written job summary statement, listing your key skills as they relate to the position you are seeking. This design is focused on presenting you as a natural fit for the position. It presents the necessary relevant background, including the industry you've worked in and the experience you bring.

This targeted format also allows you to project your abilities to do the job even if you only have related experience. Another advantage is that it is easy to modify to create a different version for each position you are applying for.

Here is an example of a targeted resume:

GARY CALVANESO

JOHN HOPKINS
Cell: (312) 339-6287 ▪ jhopkins@yahoo.com

SUMMARY

- Skilled sales and marketing manager with 10+ years' experience.
- Knowledge of U.S. and international markets with extensive patient monitoring experience in critical care, anesthesia, respiratory, disposables, and information systems in the hospital, outpatient and EMS channels.
- Creative problem solver whose success is characterized through a strong focus on customer service, sales and profitability.
- High-caliber presentation, negotiation, and organizational skills

INDUSTRY EXPERIENCE

- Medical Device (Patient Monitoring / Respiratory / Disposables – 9 years)
- PC Electromechanical (Components – 3 years)
- Start-up, Mid-Cap and Large Company experience (Strategic and tactical experience)

SELECTED ACCOMPLISHMENTS

- Led the Asia Pacific region and increased sales growth by 15% through accelerating account penetration into new and existing clients
- Increased ventilator product revenues by 12% through implementing new training and hiring initiatives
- Developed and implemented an innovative competitive sales training program which resulted in a 13% increase in patient monitoring sales
- Introduced employee recognition programs at all levels based on achievement of goals and objectives resulting in improved productivity, motivation and employee retention

EMPLOYMENT HISTORY

- Drager Medical (Respiratory)   Business Development Mgr.
- Emergent Respiratory (Respiratory)   Sales Account Executive
- Agilent Technologies (Components)   Corporate Accounts
- Nihon-Kohden (Patient Monitoring)   Asia-Pacific Mgr.-Singapore
- Smith Micro (Software)   Sales Representative

EDUCATION

- Columbia College, Columbia, MO   B.S. Degree - Marketing
- The University of Chicago   M.B.A. – Finance

There are other combinations of resumes which utilize aspects of the chronological, functional, achievement and targeted formats. Unless you are a creative, seasoned resume writer, I would recommend that you stick to one of these general formats.

When designing your resume, think about what you are trying to convey before choosing the style and layout. The first few lines of your resume are the most critical. Like any advertisement, your resume needs to grab the interest of the reader within the first 15 seconds.

Create a "Master Resume Template" for Content

To create a winning resume, start by creating a "Master Resume template" to give it structure and the look you want. The master resume should contain the most complete version of your skills, accomplishments and information.

Use this master template to create the details of all your skills and experience, then cut and paste the information in sections as you need to. This will make it easier to customize each resume for each job you apply for, rather than writing each one from scratch.

Keep in mind, this is a *working master document* and NOT something you send out to employers. **There is no such thing as a "general" resume.** Employers say that vague, general resumes don't make it to the next level. <u>**Resumes should be custom tailored to every job you seek**</u>. This includes using the same keywords that are used in the description listed for the position.

This sounds like a lot of work and it is, but this reduces the amount of non-related information and detail on jobs, especially if you choose to list jobs more than ten years old. Only use information pertinent to doing the specific job the resume is written for. The most important thing to do is to make it easy for the screener to see that you <u>match</u> the qualifications of the position.

Proofread Your Resume

According to HR departments and hiring managers, one of the top reasons to cast doubt on you as a viable candidate is by <u>finding spelling mistakes and typos</u>. The subliminal message this sends is; *"I do not pay attention to details"!* Many managers say, when they spot these, they stop reading and send it directly to the reject pile.

Unfortunately, many candidates put too much trust in MS Word's spell checker. The English language sometimes uses different spellings for the same sounding word (heterographs) which have different meanings.

For example, is it "too" or "to"? Did you mean you "lead" or "led"? Was it "you" or "your"? Did you mean "its" or "it's"? Is it "red" or "read"? These are common mistakes and MS Word is not sophisticated enough to catch all these anomalies. Seriously, what if spell check missed the fact that you misspelled your own name?

Check Grammar as Well as Spelling

Be sure to thoroughly proof read your resume to avoid mistakes. Don't just check for spelling; be sure to verify your grammar too! One candidate sent a resume with 2 sentences mixed up during the cut and paste edits. This is an unforgivable mistake and a sure way to miss out on an opportunity.

We tend to focus on documents from the beginning but try reading your resume backwards starting from the bottom, word by word, toward the top. While this sounds peculiar, this technique draws out errors you may have glossed over when you read it from the beginning to the end.

Try reading your resume out loud, sentence by sentence to find statements that don't read correctly or might not convey your original thought. The point here is proof read, proof read, proof read as mistakes can cost you an opportunity!

Submitting Resumes On-line

Keep in mind that many positions listed on websites that ask you to submit your resume online, do not correctly read resume formatting and especially, graphic design. This often causes odd characters to appear, unintentional page breaks, and spacing gaps.

To guard against this as much as possible, create a text only version of your resume. This version can easily be created using windows notepad. Again, be sure to proof read this carefully before sending or cutting and pasting.

Software Compatibility Issues

Many employers are standardized on MS Word and may request that you send your resume as an MS Word document rather than a .pdf. The problem is there may be incompatibilities between Word versions of 2003, 2007, 2010, 2013, 2016 and Word (Office 365).

Older versions of WORD may not necessarily be compatible with newer ones. As a rule, you should always create your resume using a minimum of MS WORD 2013 or higher when communicating with potential employers.

Test Your Resume

Check the effectiveness of your resume by giving it to a friend or colleague and ask them to spend 20 or 30 seconds reviewing it. After they read it, ask them what they perceive about you based on what they just read. If they cannot describe what you wanted them to, modify your resume and test it again. Repeat this process until it conveys the way you want it to.

The real test of a resume is based on employer responses. Are employers calling you back for jobs you are qualified for (excluding those you are not or under qualified for)? If your resume is not getting any results, take it back to the drawing board or seek professional resume help.

What to Avoid on Your Resume

Avoid Acronyms - One of the most common mistakes is to assume the reader knows the same things you do. Too often candidates will use acronyms for professional certifications such as "CFA" (Certified Financial Analyst) or "MCTS" (Microsoft Certified Technology Specialist).

Worse yet, some candidates list internal acronyms that were used in their last company. Considering that more and more resumes are screened by scanning machines, these will acronyms will have no meaning to the computer or entry level screeners.

Avoid Buzzwords – Steer clear of buzzwords and avoid using industry jargon to ensure that anyone reading your resume can understand your key selling points. You may want to consider using phrases from the job description as a good idea, but only if it accurately describes your background.

Some buzzwords are overused and ineffective. Chatter buzzwords like "Responsibilities include" provide an invitation to babble on about all your duties in your previous position. It is ok to let hiring managers know the types of tasks performed without all the details but focus on how you had you improved things instead of what you did.

Overused buzzwords like "utilized" and "leveraged" don't correspond well. Instead of sounding accomplished, these types of words make it appear you lack written communication skills. Insecure buzzwords like "familiar with" make you sound like you lack confidence with a skill or experience. Use words like "expertise in", "experience with" and "skilled in" to convey confidence.

Avoid using Personal Pronouns and Articles such as "I" or "me" - As a form of business communication, a resume should be well written and concise. Here is an example where "I" is used:

I reorganized the marketing department into upstream and downstream marketing which decreased time to market development for new products by 6 months

Drop the "I" and change it to:

Reorganized the marketing department into upstream and downstream marketing which decreased time to market development for new products by 6 months

Avoid Listing your Age or Personal Information - Personal information, such as your date of birth, marital status, height and weight should NOT be listed on your resume. Unless you are applying for positions in entertainment or modeling, looking outside the US or unless this information is specifically asked for, leave it out.

In many cases when you mention your age or marital status in your resume, some employers may discard it. I believe in some if not all States, it is technically illegal for a company to solicit a candidate's age, race, or marital status as part of the hiring process. Employers are usually unwilling to take a risk as a potential bias lawsuit is too costly.

Avoid stating "References Furnished Upon Request" - Employers are very aware that you can provide professional references, so there is no need to state this.

Resume Reference Lists

A reference list is an important piece for your marketing tool kit. It demonstrates that others feel you are a good employee and are willing to put their own reputation on the line by recommending you. References are not to be taken lightly. Despite a perfect search and interview, everything can tank in an instant when your references are checked and one comes out negative. Here are some reference list tips.

- **<u>Make sure you check with your references before listing them! Contact them and get their approval before sending the list.</u>**

- Update your list once or twice a year to make sure your references and contact information is still valid.

- Your list should include work associates and can include personal references. If you were a people manager, list one of your bosses, associates and employees. This will show that you were respected by the entire team, not just your boss.

Use Keywords in Your Resume

Be sure to use keywords throughout your resume (job title, etc.) to make sure your resume gets noticed in keyword searches. Determine your own keywords by reading job descriptions that interest you and include these words repeatedly in your resume.

As previously mentioned, when you apply for a specific position, customize your resume for the job. Use the same keywords listed in the job description because many employers today sort resumes using systems that search by keywords. The more keywords found in your resume that match the position, the greater the chances your resume will move to the second look pile.

Keywords that match may still give you an advantage. When you apply for a position where your keywords matched but you didn't get hired, chances are your resume may be archived in the company's storage media for future consideration.

By adding relevant keywords throughout your resume, you may be more likely to come up during an internal database candidate search. For example, use keywords such as *public relations, communications or developed social media content*. If the employer searches using a keyword such as "social media" your resume is likely to come up in the listing. To further emphasize the importance of keywords in today's digital world, we'll discuss the screening process that takes place in many companies.

Here's how a resume screening process typically works:

Your resume will most likely go through multiple layers of filtering before it actually gets to the hiring manager. If you miss what's important to any one of these steps, you can easily be passed over and eliminated.

The first look at your resume may likely be a computer scanning your resume or searching through a database of resumes that includes yours. Employers input all resumes into their database, regardless of the format it was received in (on-line application, email, scanned paper, etc.). This is referred to as *Resume Search Optimization* and is especially true for large and midsized companies.

The ability to apply on-line has made it convenient for applicants to send out lots of resumes which in turn, has created nightmares for employers. Resume blasters send unqualified applicant resumes to any job available has forced employers to screen and manage huge volumes of incoming resume traffic using resume screening and data base management.

Once resumes are received, companies can utilize a resume database to more efficiently search and find resumes with desired skill matches. The sad part of this methodology is that a mindless machine is screening candidates. It only cares about how the keywords on the resume match the keywords used in the job description.

This practice can skip over a perfectly qualified candidate simply because they lacked the matching keywords in their resume. *It is very important that you understand how essential it is to use keywords to effectively deal with this first screening.*

If you apply to a smaller company, your resume may be screened by an untrained HR clerk who also looks for specific keywords or phrases. There is a lesser chance that an experienced manager will be the one to review your resume. Unless the HR clerk spots the keywords or phrases they have been told to find, you have a good chance of being eliminated.

Resume Screening Software

The computer software that scans resumes is called an *Applicant Tracking System or ATS*. ATS computer scanning software can view and analyze volumes of resumes in seconds and determine whether your resume will get a second look. In fact, it is estimated that at least 40% of all employers now use an applicant tracking system (ATS) to screen candidates for their job openings.

These systems are designed to save employers time by recognizing strong candidates and eliminating weak ones. Sadly, the software makes a decision based on the way your resume is written, not based on the information it conveys. In fact, 75% of candidates will never have their resume looked at by a human. However inhumane this seems, it is becoming more common given the sheer volume of applicants.

If a job offer is posted via a job board, your resume will most likely be scanned by bots before it is ever actually read by a human being. Once you click the apply button, an applicant tracking system will scan your resume for the specific terms it has been given that match the job description.

The software will then quickly narrow down the applicant pool to only those candidates who best match the position description. Some ATS systems are better equipped to recognize phrases as well as keywords. The problem is, there are older exact-match systems that are still in use which will hurt your chances if you do not exactly match words.

Applicant tracking software can also be used to post job openings on a corporate website or job board, screen resumes, and generate interview requests to potential candidates by email. There are dozens of these ATS systems on the market, some are SaS applications, others are cloud based services. Some are designed for large companies and others for small to midsize companies.

The ATS system also collects and stores candidate resumes and job-related data to track and monitor the process for candidates through all stages of the hiring process. Other ATS features include pre-screening questions, source tracking, source effectiveness reports and resume process tools.

How an Applicant Tracking System Works

To ensure that your resume doesn't get filtered out on the first pass, there are several things about an ATS that you should know, including how it functions.

The applicant tracking system scans, organizes and stores resumes, allowing employers and recruiters to filter, rank, sort and track all the resumes they receive. When a resume is submitted, it is scanned using Optical Character Recognition (OCR) technology which digitizes the resume and allows it to become searchable.

While the resume is being scanned with OCR, words and letters may be unrecognized if the software has difficulty matching the expected information with the fields where specific data is stored.

For example, if you used graphic images, text boxes or tables, the ATS will have difficulty extracting data from the text boxes or tables. Worse yet, it will likely not recognize what the image is or what it represents and could make the resume look like it was poorly formatted. This is the reason why I recommend sticking with standard fonts and formats on your resume.

The ATS searches the data fields for the applicant name and contact information, work experience, job titles, employer names, dates of employment and education. For each job posting, the ATS searches data fields for specific keywords and phrases associated with the position.

The software will look to match the data on the resume with fields in the specified in the software. If your resume doesn't contain these specific keywords or phrases, it will most likely be filtered out for rejection. Once the resume is rejected, the system may be programmed to generate an automated rejection response message which is emailed to the applicant.

The ATS is designed to rank resumes on various types of criteria. For example, a resume that is considered a strong match for the job posting requirements might be based on the frequency that the keywords and phrases appear.

Another downside of ATS use is that hiring managers and recruiters rarely see the actual resume unless you get invited in for an interview. They typically see an ATS screen view showing the information in the database that the software pulled out of the resume.

Beating the ATS Resume Readers

Take heart, there is a way to improve your chances with these types of resume readers. Here are some ideas to help increase the odds of getting past the ATS computer gatekeepers:

1. First rule! - **don't apply if you are not qualified!** You might get past the computer, but you will be rejected by the first pair of human eyes. If you are not even remotely qualified, don't waste their time or yours.

2. Before sending your resume on-line in word format, locate the job description from the posting

3. Highlight and copy keyword text from the job posting

4. Paste them into your resume in areas that you have similar skills, so the keywords and phrases interspersed into the text. This takes wordsmithing and a lot of attention to detail.

When the computer scans your resume for the keywords or phrases, it will flag your resume as one that could potentially meet the qualifications. This may at least get you a second look by a human. You still must be qualified to move along in the process!

Beware, some companies program their software to reject an exact word match, so you may want to modify the job description text or just capture the key words or phrases to get past the software.

The first resume look - Since the first resume look may not be by a human being, it is important to understand the process so you can maximize your chances of getting past the first look. Larger companies receive hundreds if not thousands of resumes for each position posted and they do not have enough people to screen this initial volume of resumes.

The second resume look – Assuming you used the matching keywords and were selected in the search, your resume will move on to the next level.

Only the top 2-3% of matching resumes move on to a human being. This may be the first level of human screening before passing your resume along with other resumes to be reviewed by the hiring manager. This step may be assigned to a clerk or HR generalist.

Unfortunately, low level HR clerks do not have any type of experience understanding the job or expertise they are screening resumes for. The clerk's role is to manually sort and review resumes for a variety of positions in the company.

In a single day, they may screen and review hundreds of resumes, spending approximately 15 seconds on each. What they are looking for is to match your skills to the job description! They are verifying that the computer got it right and do not want to send unqualified candidates to the hiring manger. Here again, this re-emphasizes the importance of using keywords in your resume.

The third resume look – If you have made it this far, congratulations! You have a real shot at moving forward in the process. A hiring manager will receive about 10 – 15 resumes from HR and will usually select 2 or 3 for serious consideration / an interview. Here again, the hiring manager is looking for the keywords and phrases on your resume that match the skills they envision are needed for the job.

Keep in mind that if you are selected to be interviewed based on your resume, <u>the hiring manager already believes you are qualified</u>. Too many candidates go into interviews believing that they need to sell the manager on their job knowledge. While we devote an entire chapter to interviewing, it is mostly about making a human and cultural connection with the hiring manager.

The last resume look – Depending on the company and culture, it is a common practice for a hiring manager to ask his or her boss to review the top resumes selected for potential interviews. Again, this is will only be 2 or 3 at most.

This is a practice of selling up and can be used to get advance buy-in from the boss in the event the selected candidate does not work out. The resume may also be reviewed by the hiring manager's peers or team members to get consensus from valued members of the team.

Summary - Resume Do's and Don'ts:

Do

1. **Do** create some form of professional or executive summary at the top of your resume followed by a list of bulleted achievements or qualifications. Make sure that you customize this with keywords and phrases taken from the job description in context.

2. **Do** be honest on your resume. Exaggerations and lies will create problems for you later especially if you get hired (and you will most likely be fired). False statements may be found during a background check.

3. **Do** list your accomplishments, not a step by step summary of what you did for each job. Employers want to know what makes you stand out from the crowd. Tell them how you saved them money, increased their efficiency, or reduced their costs.

4. **Do** list your accomplishments in quantifiable terms. Tell the employer how you saved dollars or time, improved services, exceeded objectives, improved efficiency, etc.

5. **Do** use action verbs to describe the points you want to make. Saying you are "*A web designer*" is far less impressive than telling the reader that you *"Design cutting edge and modern websites"*.

6. **Do** limit your employment history to the past 10-12 years. Unfortunately, age discrimination is alive and well and can be an obstacle for older workers. A well-crafted resume is the tool that can get you into the employment door for that initial interview. Point out what makes you stand out from younger applicants; your judgment and decision-making abilities, your experience and range of expertise, your dependable work ethic and your understanding and commitment to achieving corporate goals.

7. **Do** check for misspellings. If you apply online for jobs, keep in mind that misspelled keywords will most likely be missed by the ATS, producing fewer matches and will lower your ranking.

8. **Do** make sure your resume looks professional and polished, but not overwhelmingly graphic.

9. **Do** have your resume critiqued by someone else, preferably a professional career coach or a friend. An investment in creating a top-notch resume is surely worth the money.

10. **Do** fill in all the information requested as required for the application process, even if it requests including your resume. Not responding may be used to filter you out by a screener.

Don'ts

1. **Don't** bother applying for positions that don't really match your experience and skills. You are wasting your time and the employers.

2. **Don't** use slang words, acronyms that are not relative or abbreviations such as "Mgmt" instead of "Management" especially if you apply for jobs on-line. ATS systems are not programmed for these terms. They are looking for the exact keywords.

3. **Don't** list the specific year you graduated from college if you are an older candidate. Just list the school and the degree. A general rule is to omit college graduation / other educational dates that are over 20 years old unless you are seeking a top-level management position.

4. **Don't** include hobbies or other similar items unless it specifically relates to the position. For example, a non-profit company might be interested in your charitable or volunteer work with a similar organization.

5. **Don't** list your prior salary on your resume.

6. **Don't** use fancy resume templates which include background graphics, photos, or logos. If you apply on-line, they can confuse the information processed by the ATS.

7. **Don't** use non-standard or unusual fonts. Stick with basic fonts like Arial or Times New Roman, never smaller than #10 font and not larger than #12 font unless it's a header. Keep in mind that the person or ATS reviewing your resume needs to have the same default fonts on their computer otherwise your resume may not be readable or look like it was not properly formatted.

8. **Don't** send your resume out as an attachment when applying on-line in an email. As a precaution to avoid being filtered by security scans, cut and paste it into the body of the e-mail.

9. **Don't** include "references upon request" on your resume as they expect you will provide this information when asked. Prepare your reference list and have it available (using the same font/format as your resume).

10. **Don't** forget to include a cover letter when applying to a smaller company. A strong cover letter can separate you from the other candidates.

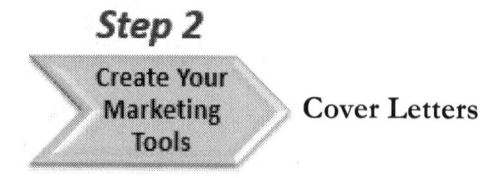

Step 2: Create Your Marketing Tools — **Cover Letters**

Chapter 8

COVER LETTERS THAT GET ATTENTION

I will start by saying that cover letters are NOT as important as they used to be. In fact, most recruiters don't even open a cover letter attachment, nor do they even give cover letters a passing glance. Since the number of resume reading Applicant Tracking Systems (ATS) has increased, many companies don't bother with cover letters. Many companies have even stopped asking for them.

Bottom line, if you are applying for jobs online, the chances of your cover letter being looked at are slim. If you attach both a cover letter AND a resume in the email, only the resume will likely get read. In cases where employers are using an ATS system (especially in tech companies), your cover letter will most likely be ignored.

When Should You Send a Cover Letter?

So if cover letters are a dying breed, candidates often ask if or when should they send a cover letter? You should send a cover letter whenever you communicate directly with a hiring manager or when applying to a small company. Small companies that cannot afford ATS systems typically read cover letters because they still sort and file resumes manually. (This may soon change as basic, low cost ATS systems are entering the market).

When you "target" a company (covered in an upcoming chapter), *the contact point is the hiring manager* and anytime you communicate directly with a hiring manager, a cover letter should be sent along with a resume. This also applies when applying for management consulting or senior level positions.

The cover letter gives the manager a chance to read a brief summary about you. It may be the first thing the employer reads, even before the resume. Just like a resume; a cover letter should be customized to the position.

Like the resume, the purpose of a cover letter is to emphasize that you have the skills and qualifications that match the specified requirements. This makes it easy for the screener or hiring manager to see that you are a good fit for the position and move you along in the process. If your cover letter reads like everyone else's, it's more likely your resume will not be read.

Where Should You Send a Cover Letter?

Where and to whom you send it to depends on the position and how you applied. Sending a cover letter and resume directly to the hiring manager or head of the specific department will get you the best chance of being read.

Typically, resumes are addressed to HR (Human Resources). If you include a cover letter to HR, the cover letter may not even be read. This is especially true if you apply online and the resume goes through an automated ATS review.

If you don't know the hiring managers name, do the research! Make calls to the company and ask. Search LinkedIn and other internet sources for the names of someone you know that might be able to help. Check with your network groups to see if someone knows the hiring managers name.

After thoroughly researching, if the hiring managers' name is still unknown, use a title such as VP Engineering, Director Purchasing, VP Sales, etc. However, the manager may still forward it to Human Resources.

What Happens When You Don't Send a Cover Letter

Sending resumes without cover letters has become the norm for online applications unless they are specifically requested. When you submit a resume <u>directly to a hiring manager</u> without a cover letter, you lose the opportunity to deliver a targeted summary directly to the person who might hire you.

If your cover letter is provided to the hiring manager in an email, the subject line should always list the job title and reference number. As we discussed earlier, don't communicate with a potential employer using an e-mail address such as "valleygirl22@gmail.com or "dude73@yahoo.com. Employers may find this immature and not take you seriously.

Show That You Understand Facts About the Company

One way to really impress an employer is to show that you have knowledge about what the company does and its mission / vision. Study the company and get educated! Go to the company's website and read all about them.

Search the internet for additional information on the company. What do financial analysts, customers and employees say about them? Learn what the company makes or services. Show them that you understand their business and it will make you more valuable.

Short and to the Point

Many applicants make the same mistake in the cover letter, rambling on about their fantastic skills and experience. Employers are far too busy to read long and detailed letters that don't address their issues. Short and to the point is better.

Highlight Your Most Important Attributes That Match the Needs of the Employer

It's not about you. It's about the needs of the employer and how well your skills match. Closely review the job description - Write about how your accomplishments map to the job requirements. Focus your cover letter on the specific experience and skills in your resume that are required for the position.

Be Enthusiastic

In your cover letter, demonstrate your eagerness to adapt in the company culture. Employers want candidates that are positive, enthusiastic and passionate about their work. Show that you are eager to take on new responsibilities and give them something that sets you apart from the field. Get creative!

What Makes a Good Cover Letter?

So, what makes a good cover letter that gets attention? Start by <u>taking the time</u> to write a good one! Write the cover letter in the same way you would want to receive it if you were the employer. Focus on the key attributes that are relative to the job and the industry. Use language and terminology that speaks directly to the reviewer. This will ensure they understand you are a good match for what they are looking for.

In small companies, HR staffs are small so they don't have a lot of time to sort and arrange resumes. Providing the title and reference number on your cover letter ensures your information will be connected with the correct open position.

Cover Letter Examples

Ideally, you'll be sending your cover letter directly to the hiring manager. Use the first paragraph to make an introduction explaining who you are and what you are looking for. Here are some examples of this type of cover letter text:

Example #1: I am writing to express my interest in the (JOB TITLE) position and have attached my resume for your review. With over 4 years of successes in sales management roles, I am confident that I can make a valuable contribution to your organization's sales related goals and initiatives.

Example #2: I am a highly motivated (STATE YOUR FUNCTIONAL EXPERTISE – Finance, Engineering, etc.) manager with a solid track record of accomplishments. I have taken the liberty of attaching my resume to introduce myself as my background may be of interest. I would welcome the opportunity to speak further with you about your (JOB TITLE) position.

Example #3: I am responding to your (POSTING or ADVERTISEMENT) in the (NAME OF JOB BOARD, WEBSITE or PUBLICATION) for a (JOB TITLE). The job requirements appear to be an excellent match for my related experience and skills. Please find enclosed my resume for your review and consideration.

Example #4: I would like to apply for your (JOB TITLE) position. As a quality-focused professional with a consistent record of meeting and exceeding employer requirements, I would like to present my resume for your consideration.

Example #5: Your listing for a (JOB TITLE) captured my interest. I am currently seeking new employment opportunities and would like to take this opportunity to introduce myself. Please find enclosed my resume for your review and consideration.

Example #6: In response to your ad for a (JOB TITLE) advertised in the (NAME OF JOB BOARD, WEBSITE or PUBLICATION), I am submitting my resume. (Develop an overview statement here that summarizes your strengths, experiences, knowledge for the position, and how these attributes benefit the company/position.)

Poor Grammar

Here is an example of what **NOT TO DO**! Note the difference between my previous examples and the following. The example below is filled with run on sentences, poor grammar and confusing messages. It also sounds desperate.

"Regarding your listing for a customer service rep, I am responding to your posting and hope you will take time to consider me for the customer service job, as I have almost 5 years of doing this same job at another company. I hope you will choose to interview me as I have already been in this type of job before and know exactly how to do it. I can provide you with more information about this if you need it. I would appreciate your consideration as I have been unemployed for four months and would like to go back to work asap. I am very confident I can do the job day one".

Your cover letter should demonstrate good grammar and should convey that you are a person that communicates well. Be specific about what job you are seeking, state your qualifications, and request an opportunity to meet in person.

There are a several styles of cover letters that can be used to communicate your value. Here are two of the most common styles; **skills** and **interest** cover letters.

Skills Cover Letter

A *Skills* cover letters provides an effective way to communicate how well your qualifications match the job requirements. Using a point by point comparison, the skill cover letter compares the specification of the position to your actual experience or skills.

Be sure to use the same words and terminology the company used in the job description. Provide 4 to 6 bulleted points to convey how your skills match. Most of all, customize this section to the specifics of every job you apply for.

The following is an example of a *Skills Cover Letter*:

Subject: Job Title & Reference #

Dear (MR. /MS. LAST NAME):

I am writing to express my interest in the (JOB NAME) position and have attached my resume for your review. With over 8 years of successes in sales leadership roles, I am confident that I can make a valuable contribution to your organization's sales related goals and initiatives. Since the candidate description appears to be an excellent match for my related experience and skills, I have taken the liberty to pointing out how my skills and experience match the requirements of the position.

Position Requirement	**My Qualifications**
Start-up Experience	2 successful startup ventures
Built Sales Organizations	Hired, coached, mentored successful sales teams
Sales Management Experience	3 yrs as a sales manager
5+ yrs in Medical Device Industry	6 yrs experience in Medical Device
3+ yrs in Cardiology sales	5 yrs in Cardiology and Cardiovascular products

Considering the similarity between my qualifications and the specifications for the position, I would appreciate the opportunity for a personal meeting. I believe it would be both interesting and mutually beneficial. I look forward to speaking with you.

Sincerely,

Your Name
Phone: (XXX) – XXX-XXXX
Email: XXXXX@XXX.com

Skills Cover Letter Contents

The *skills* cover letter style should provide the following:

1. An introduction to who you are, preferably in the first paragraph

2. A listing of the key job requirements

3. A listing of how your qualifications meet the key job requirements

4. Ask for a meeting

Interests Cover Letter

The *interests'* cover letter is traditional and descriptive in format. Its purpose is to show that you bring the expertise needed for the position. As you do for a resume, learn about the company by researching articles in news publications and through trade magazines.

Researching the industry will help you write what is relevant to the employer. You might include industry related details, such as a problem the company, market or the industry is facing. Use keywords and phrases that are familiar to the employer or the industry to demonstrate that you understand the issues and could contribute to resolving them.

Another idea is to congratulate them on a newly received contract or recent merger as part of your cover letter. Mergers often shuffle out current employees and create new openings. Winning new contracts also means more revenue and provides job openings. This too shows that you are knowledgeable about the company and have done your research.

The interests cover letter can be used to combine the key points from your resume into the cover letter. Use the most relevant accomplishments from your resume and list them in bulleted form. Don't use long sentences or paragraphs. Whenever possible, keep the letter to one page. Be clear and concise about what you are looking to convey.

As I have mentioned a few times, use the marketing principle of communication that less is more. Think of your messaging in terms of a *"billboard" not a "bulletin board"*. Conclude your letter by stating that you are a good fit for the job and request an opportunity to discuss the position further with them.

Here is an Example of an Interests Cover Letter

Subject: Job Title & Reference #

Dear (MR. /MS. LAST NAME):

I would like to apply for your (JOB TITLE) position. As a quality-focused professional with a consistent record of meeting and exceeding requirements, I would like to present my resume for your consideration.

The following is a summarization of my qualifications to demonstrate how my skills and experience meet the job requirements as specified:

- _____

(Short statements)

- _____

- _____

- _____

Thank you for taking the time to review my credentials. I would appreciate an opportunity to speak with you to further discuss the position. Please let me know when you might be available. I have provided my contact information below.

Sincerely,

Your Name
Phone: (XXX) – XXX-XXXX
Email: XXXXX@XXX.com

Interests Cover Letter Contents

The *interests'* cover letter style should provide the following:

1. Start with brief overview of yourself in the context of how the job is described, preferably in the first paragraph.

2. Demonstrate that your skills match what the company is looking for, letting them know you are well qualified for the position.

3. Point out that you are very interested in the position and would like to pursue it vigorously.

4. The *interests'* cover letter is written in the first person; "I" and "me".

Cover Letter Explain Gaps in Your Resume

A cover letter can also be used to explain quirks or gaps in your resume. Unfortunately, too many candidates miss the opportunity to use their cover letter to explain gaps or unusual circumstances. Without clarification, your resume may be rejected simply from misunderstanding.

For example, let's say you were a working mother who took 5 years off to raise your child. Even though you were a proven performer and took time off, your resume shows a 5-year gap without explanation.

Without an explanation, the employer may surmise that must be some reason that you were unemployed and no one would hire you for 5 years. Employers prefer to avoid risks and unexplained resume gaps give them reason for concern.

This is yet another reason why generic cover letters are ineffective and don't work. Customize your cover letter for every job you apply for. Use words from the job description and point out how the needs relate to your skills and experience. Address the specific interests of the company.

Keep Your Cover Letter Friendly

When you are writing a cover letter, put your personality in it as if you were speaking directly to the reader. You are speaking directly to the hiring manager so don't make your cover letter too formal.

Personalize the cover letter but make it short and to the point. Be respective of the employers' time. Along with conveying your skills and experience, let the employer know you appreciate how busy they are. Say something like; "I really appreciate the time you've given, considering how busy you are".

Don't Talk about Salary or Salary Requirements

Unless it was specifically requested by an employer, this is not the time to start a discussion about salary. You haven't even been considered for the position. Focus on presenting your skills and accomplishments related to the position and leave the salary discussion to when you receive an offer.

Be Honest

Too many candidates exaggerate their credentials. Focus on your strengths and accomplishments without being dishonest. While being honest, a cover letter is not the place to state that you were laid off, fired, or had some other issue.

Don't forget to provide your contact information.

Forgetting to provide your own contact information is more common than you think. Candidates will put their phone number and e-mail address on the cover letter, but not their resume and vice versa. Too often, I have seen it left off of both!

All cover letters should include an e-mail address and phone number at the end of the correspondence. When you don't, it sends a subliminal message to the employer that you don't pay attention to details.

Proofread

Just as you would for a resume, proofread for grammatical errors, typos and spelling mistakes. Don't rely on MS Word to fix your mistakes! Pay careful attention to font size and consistency. Don't cram more information onto your cover letter by using smaller fonts.

No one is going to read a lot of information in 20 seconds. As we did with the resume, always create your cover letter in MS Word for paper mailers and in notepad for e-mail submissions. This will ensure there are no weird computer related characters for the reader.

Proof reading is so important. Mistakes can cost you an opportunity! Use a friend or colleague to check the effectiveness of your cover letter. Use the 20 second test and ask them to tell you what it says. If they cannot describe what you wanted to convey, modify your cover letter and test it again. Repeat this process until they can describe exactly what you expected them to take away.

Focus on Follow-up

Be aggressive and ask for an appointment. Tell the employer that you are planning to make a follow-up call and provide an exact date within the next few days. Be sure to follow through and call on the date and time you said you would. Employers like to know that you really want the position.

Closing Statements in a Cover Letter.

How you end your cover letter is just as important as how you start it. By creating a first-class closing statement, you are showing the hiring manager that you are confident, professional, and polite. It also shows that you really want the job. Here are some examples:

Example #1: Please find additional details regarding my career accomplishments in the attached resume. I would appreciate an opportunity to discuss the needs of your organization. I am confident it will be interesting and mutually beneficial. Thank you in advance for your time and consideration.

Example #2: I have taken the liberty of enclosing my resume for your review. I think you will agree that my skills and expertise are very relevant the (NAME OF COMPANY)'s products and services. I would welcome an opportunity for a personal interview to discuss how I might address the needs of your organization.

Example #3: Thank you in advance for taking the time to review my credentials. I would appreciate the opportunity for a personal meeting and am available at your convenience. If you have any questions, please call me.

Example #4: To follow-up on this letter of inquiry, I will contact next week (specify a date). If you have any questions or require any additional information, please contact me. Thank you again for your consideration.

Example #5: After you have had an opportunity to review my credentials, I would appreciate an opportunity to discuss my background in greater detail with you. Please let me know when I might be able to contact you. My contact information is listed below.

Step 2
Create Your Marketing Tools

Your LinkedIn Profile

Chapter 9

USING LINKEDIN IN YOUR JOB SEARCH

Currently, the number one on-line tool for job search and business social networking is LinkedIn. **It is the single most important marketing tool for the job seeker!**

LinkedIn has completely reinvented the process of business networking, especially for those interested in career change. LinkedIn's platform allows anyone to socially network with hiring companies, find new jobs and most importantly, be found by potential employers.

Just posting your credentials on LinkedIn's social platform can reach massive audiences anywhere in the business world. This is a paradigm shift from the past, allowing employers to search for candidates and recruit them, whether or not they are employed.

LinkedIn's platform also allows users to easily keep their contact and profile information current. This makes it even easier for employers to find potential candidate information. It also provides companies with the most up to date contact information on potential business clients. With a tool this powerful, even the most diehard, hold out senior executives now recognize the importance of being listed on LinkedIn.

LinkedIn became a public company in 2011 and was purchased by Microsoft in 2016 for $26.2 Billion dollars! As of this writing, LinkedIn has become the world's largest social business network with more than 590 million members in over 200 countries / territories and is available in 24 different languages. After the United States, India, Brazil, Great Britain and Canada have the highest number of LinkedIn users.

For business, 61 million LinkedIn users are senior level influencers and 40 million are in decision-making positions. No other social media platform has as much business influence.

Candidate Searches

According to LinkedIn's research, 87% of all recruiters use LinkedIn to search or vet candidates. Most of these recruiting firms subscribe to LinkedIn's premium paid subscription services which allows them greater access to candidate details. So do many hiring managers. In fact, it has become common place for HR departments to search LinkedIn for candidates with specific skills and experience.

Knowing this, it's important that you have a complete, on-line profile actively available for viewing on LinkedIn. The more relevant the content you provide in your profile, the higher the probability someone will locate you during a candidate search. The opposite is also true as hiring managers are less likely to find candidates whose profiles are sparse or incomplete!

Increase Your Personal Brand and Visibility

For the job seeker, LinkedIn provides a powerful tool to increase your personal brand visibility. With its massive social reach, you can build an army of professional contacts, obtain recommendation and endorsements, join groups and even develop a reputation as a subject matter expert.

Increase Your Personal Brand Visibility

Build & Strengthen Profile
- Brand & Value Proposition
- Get Found - Keywords

Create A Target Company List
- Leverage Internal Connections
- Pass Your Resume to Hiring Managers

Meet People
- Increase Your Network
- Increase Your Visibility

Join Groups
- Attend Meetings
- Become Subject Matter Expert

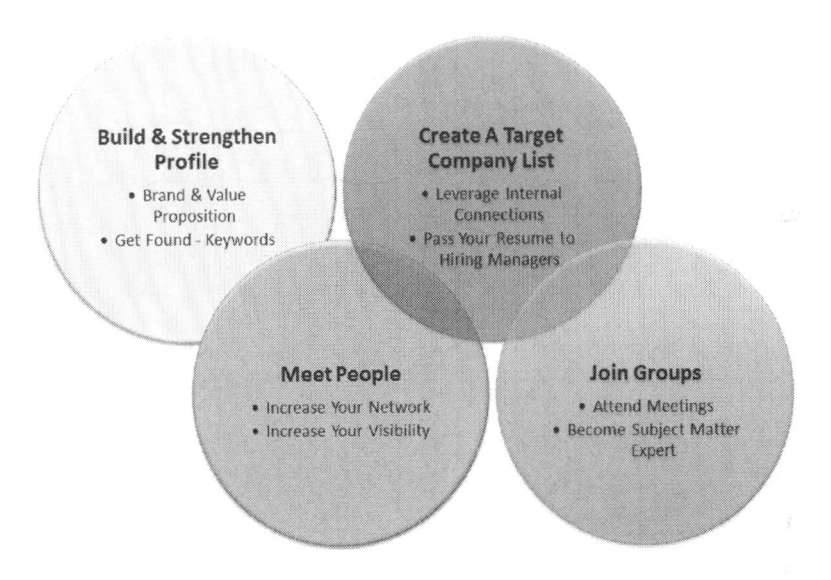

Figure 9-1: Increase Your Personal Brand and Visibility

Comparing LinkedIn and Facebook

While Facebook was the world's first social networking platform, it wasn't initially designed for business. To increase its revenue, Facebook added functionality to allow companies to create business related pages and sell advertising. Facebook also makes a significant amount of its revenue by selling mountains of personal information that it collects. It sells this information to marketing firms and various businesses for targeted advertising.

LinkedIn was designed for a different purpose; to socially connect business people and find business related resources. Since Microsoft's purchase of LinkedIn, Microsoft has revamped LinkedIn's main feed, modeling it to look more like Facebook's with trending stories and posts from contacts. Just like Facebook, you can unfollow and hide posts easily.

Free vs. Paid Subscription

LinkedIn has also changed its search interface capabilities. Microsoft reduced the number of "free version" capabilities and added features to their paid subscription-based services. These changes have reduced the functionality of the "free" version and its ability to search for jobs, people, companies and to connect with other subscribers.

Let's not forget that first and foremost, LinkedIn is a business that wants to make money! As the leading business social networking site, LinkedIn has become an invaluable job search tool. With millions of users and their multiple levels of connections, LinkedIn knows they offer the best on-line place for hiring managers to search for talent.

While you can get away with simply using the "free" profile to post your resume and search for jobs, to leverage all the capabilities of LinkedIn, you'll need to pay for a monthly subscription. LinkedIn not only offers premium services for job seekers, but also offers other types of premium business subscription services.

LinkedIn's Premium Packages for Job Seekers

While their offerings, pricing and capabilities consistently change, as of this writing, these are the premium services offered by LinkedIn:

- **Premium Career** – for job seekers looking to get hired or change careers

- **Sales Navigator** – used to generate leads and build clientele.

- **Recruiter Lite** – used by recruiters and HR to find and hire talent.

- **Premium Business** – provides detailed business insights to expand your business

- **LinkedIn Learning** – To improve existing skills and learn new ones.

For the job seeker, LinkedIn's **Premium Career** subscription provides you with the following enhanced capabilities:

- **Access to expert career coaches -** Get answers & advice via a private online community staffed with career support experts

- **Direct messaging** - Reach out directly to any recruiter or job poster with 5 "InMail" credits - InMail capability allows you to reach out directly to contact recruiters, hiring managers or respond to job postings. This means you can contact anyone on LinkedIn, regardless of the degree of separation.

- **Who's Viewed Your Profile** - See who's viewed you in the last 90 days and how they found you. This feature lets you know when someone has been looking at your profile. While the free members can only see the last few viewers, premium subscribers can see all viewers.

- **Featured Applicant** - Shows your profile as a "Featured Applicant" to move to the top of recruiters' applicant lists. When your application hits the job poster's inbox along with other candidates, you come in at the top of the list to get a first look from the screener. Any LinkedIn member can see your profile and reach out to you. Helps you to stand out to recruiters when you apply as a featured applicant

- **Applicant Insights** allows you to see how you compare to other candidates. This will help you better understand how you compare to other candidates with similar backgrounds. When you locate a job posting at one of your target companies, you can use the Applicant Insight feature to visualize how you compare to other applicants by skills, education, seniority level, education, etc.

- **Instant access to salary insights** - See salary details when browsing jobs without sharing your personal data

- **Online video courses**

Since the price of an upgrade to premium job seeker is constantly changing, you'll need to review what it currently is and consider whether you feel it is worth the cost. I suggest at a minimum, you try it out free for 30 days. Why not? You have nothing to lose and everything to gain.

Are the Premium Services Worth It?

Opinions vary, and some people feel strongly that its worth every dollar while other disagree. For job search candidates, I believe it is absolutely necessary if you are looking to for a job or looking to change careers.

I have found that most of the power networkers I know use the premium services. Keep in mind that LinkedIn constantly changes its prices, features and offerings, so these capabilities are only valid as of the writing of this book.

LinkedIn's Social Network and Degrees of Connection

To help you understand just how powerful LinkedIn is for your job search, it is important to understand its social media reach. LinkedIn provides a means to "link" with other professionals in what it calls "connections". The total number of connections you have is called your "network" and your network is made up of what LinkedIn calls its 1st degree, 2nd degree and 3rd degree connections.

1st degree connections are people you have directly connected with because they have accepted an invitation to connect request from you or you have accepted theirs. You can communicate with them by sending a message through LinkedIn.

2nd degree connections are people that are connected to your 1st degree connections but are not directly with you. You can send them an invitation to connect or contact them through LinkedIn's internal email system called "InMail".

3rd degree connections are people that are connected to your 2nd degree connections but again are not directly with you. How you can connect with them varies. You can only connect with them through InMail.

Why is this important?

The more people that are in your 1st, 2nd and 3rd degrees of separation, the more times your name will show up in a search. As an example, let's assume you have made 500, 1st degree connections (*which LinkedIn considers a key milestone for the number for connections in your profile*). 500 connections would link you to over 5 million people on LinkedIn through your 2nd and 3rd degree connections. With that many connections, LinkedIn can change your life's career path, especially if you are considering a job change or are searching for a new job!

Join LinkedIn

If you don't already have an account setup with LinkedIn, it is very important to create your own on-line profile and keep it current. While I can make suggestions in setting up your on-line profile, it would be futile to provide step by step instructions since LinkedIn regularly changes its pages, flow and services.

Be sure to set up an on-line profile which reflects your resume / personal brand information discussed in earlier chapters. This profile information should be tailored toward the type of position you are looking for. Make sure your profile is always up to date with your current skills and accomplishments as well as previous positions. Whether you are employed or not, LinkedIn is the way to market your professional experience and skills and get found.

Your LinkedIn Profile

Here are some important elements to help you set up your profile:

- ☐ **Headline** - Create a keyword rich "Headline" that reflects the job you are after and what you want to be known for on LinkedIn. For example, if you are a *"Marketing Manager"*, make sure that or similar title is reflected in your header. You can also include a tag-line to reflect your value and how you want to be known; e.g. *"Helping businesses build and promote lasting brands."* Make sure you include your full name. Using a first name with a last initial is not sufficient for searches. You want to make this headline area memorable! Again, be sure to include search keywords in this section.

- ☐ **Photo** - Be sure to post a professional looking photo of you. I have seen many people avoid posting a photo on their LinkedIn profile out of a concern that their employer will see it and think you are looking for a job. This is a common mistake. Most employers generally accept that their employees have LinkedIn business profiles. In fact, most of the managers do too! If you are concerned about privacy, you are more likely to be seen on Facebook than LinkedIn. If you don't have a photo, potential employers may question why you don't, making it easier to skip by you as a candidate. In fact, according to LinkedIn, you are 7 times more likely to be found in searches if you have a professional photo!

- **Summary** - Create a "Summary" of you so that employers read about your strengths first and the kind of results you can bring as a business professional. You should have already developed a summary for your resume and LinkedIn will provide you with the space to articulate it in more detail. *(Again, think billboard, not bulletin board!)* The summary should highlight your personal brand/ value proposition to include skills, experience, expertise and style. It can also be used to describe your aspirations. Also, be sure to keyword your summary so you rank higher in searches. Special skills are a great for specific keyword searches.

- **Personalized URL** - Edit your LinkedIn URL (Universal Resource Link) to create your unique public profile URL for LinkedIn. In the header section of LinkedIn, click on the gear symbol which will allow you to edit your public profile. As a default, your LinkedIn URL contains a lot of extra characters. You should change this to a URL that includes your name. e.g. www.linkedin.com/in/yourname.

- **Job Titles** - Provide current and past titles. Provide a thorough work history of each role and fill it with your keywords. As you did with the resume, use accomplishments.

- **Education** - Provide your educational background including degrees, certifications, etc. Add all the colleges you have attended along with advanced training. This is especially important if you are right out of college with little professional work experience.
- **Skills & Expertise** – Provide at least 5 key skills on your prole.
- **Location & Industry** - Add your industry and ZIP code so recruiters looking for local candidates can find you.
- **Add email addresses** - Provide at least 2 email addresses to avoid accidentally losing access to your account.
- **Make Yourself Stand Out** - Add a "human" touch. For example, volunteer work, which might be relevant. Stay away from statements or comments regarding political affiliations and / or religion unless you are pursuing positions in those areas.
- **Recommendations and Endorsements** - Another great feature on LinkedIn is its ability to highlight on-line recommendations about you. LinkedIn does this in 2 different ways; *recommendations and endorsements*.

Recommendations are basically letters of reference posted on your profile by others. These can include former bosses, colleagues, clients and even friends. Your profile should have a minimum of 3 recommendations. However, I recommend having 4 to 8. You also have the ability screen the recommendations and decide whether or not they should be posted. Ask former colleagues, clients, managers, and classmates to write *recommendations* on your profile but DON'T reciprocate writing recommendations for them! An employer can easily see that a person recommended you and you recommended them back which negates the value of the recommendation.

Endorsements provide a method to be recognized by your 1st-degree connections' skills. Your connections can validate strengths found on your profile and you can endorse others with one-click. Skill endorsements are a simple way of building your professional brand and engaging others in your network. Here again, ask former colleagues, clients, managers, and classmates to provide *endorsements* on your profile. But unlike recommendations, you can reciprocate and endorse skills for others. One of the flaws of endorsements is that people that barely know you may endorse you for a skill that you may or may not have. They may perceive you have this skill when you really don't. This flaw diminishes the validity of endorsements. Conversely, sheer numbers of people endorsing you for a specific skill or skills shows core competencies in your profile. Multiple endorsements can go a long way in helping you establish your professional brand. Some more than others. For example, an endorsement from an existing colleague is more valuable to a recruiter or hiring manager than a similar endorsement from a personal friend. Keep this in mind when you endorse others.

- **Volunteer Experience** – Be sure to list your experience as a volunteer. According to LinkedIn, 42% of hiring managers surveyed said they view volunteer experience equal to formal work experience.
- **Website Links** - You can add up to 3 website links to your profile. Some ideas to consider are links to your professional blog, twitter account, company website, etc.
- **Privacy Settings** - Be sure to check your privacy settings and contact levels searched by others. You control what others see about you and what types of notifications are sent out to your network. For example, you can set your privacy settings to *not send a*

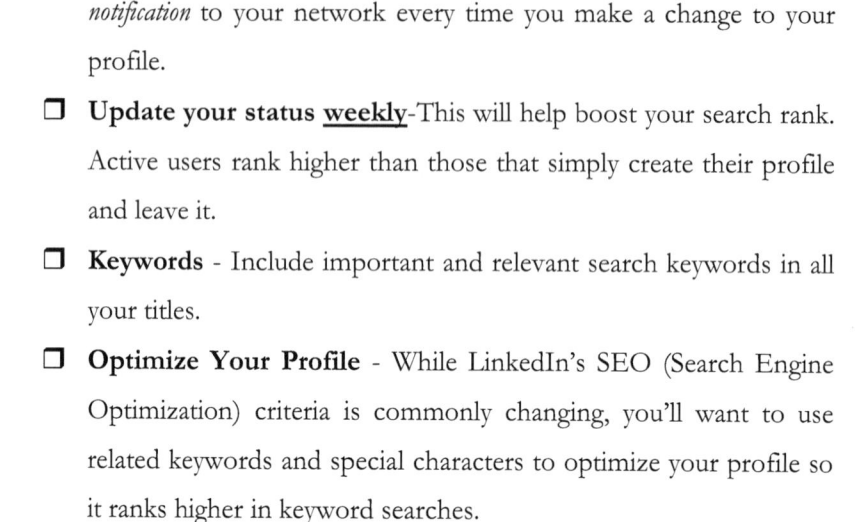

notification to your network every time you make a change to your profile.

- **Update your status <u>weekly</u>**-This will help boost your search rank. Active users rank higher than those that simply create their profile and leave it.
- **Keywords** - Include important and relevant search keywords in all your titles.
- **Optimize Your Profile** - While LinkedIn's SEO (Search Engine Optimization) criteria is commonly changing, you'll want to use related keywords and special characters to optimize your profile so it ranks higher in keyword searches.

Build Your Connections

Once your profile is setup and complete, you'll want to add connections to your network. Start with friends and family by sending connection invitations to them using the "connect" feature in LinkedIn.

Search for the names of former colleagues, supervisors, industry contacts, etc. and invite them to connect with you. Whenever possible, send them wording as a personalized invitation.

When you attend business meetings, tradeshows, network events, etc. and exchange business cards, use their business card information to send those people invitations to connect. You never know who they know and they may be the one who provides the connection for your next job.

Keep Building to Reach 500 Connections

Your target number of 1st level connections should be 500 or more. While that sounds like a lot, it is very attainable if you work at it. From LinkedIn's perspective, once you hit 500+ people, you reach a plateau which offers a number of advantages:

Search Advantage – When someone has 500 or more connections, the theory is that when a contact has credible connection with someone they have in common, they are more likely to trust you than they would with someone who does not.

Credibility – When someone with 500 or more connections comes up in a search, they instantly gain more credibility because the searcher assumes they are an established professional in their field. If they are looking for someone with a skill, product or service, they will most like go with you as the more credible connection.

Audience Reach - The more 1st level connection you have, the more likely people will see your posts and share them. Here again the theory is the more people that see your posts, the more likely they are to share them. Sharing is an important criteria in building SEO ranking for social media.

Invitations and Views – The more connections you have, the more views and invitations you will receive. Some will find you through your postings and articles and others may find you through comments made. The more views of your profile the higher you will rank in searches!

LION's

Speaking of super connectors, as with any social network there are networkers with vast amounts of connections. In the world of LinkedIn, LION stands for **LI**nkedIn **O**pen **N**etworker. "L.I.O.N." is a designation used by several user-created groups and individual LinkedIn members to indicate a high level of interconnectivity to other LinkedIn members. Keep in mind, some people believe you should only connect to people you know and trust and only join groups you want your name associated with.

Groups and Associations

Another method to add social connections to your LinkedIn account is through Groups and Associations.

LinkedIn Groups allow professionals in the same industry or that have similar interests to communicate and post information. Most groups provide discussion forums, job boards and news. They share content, find answers, post and view jobs, make business contacts, etc. Those that post as part of the group, become content authors often establish themselves as industry experts. I recommend that you join the maximum number of groups that LinkedIn allows which, as of this writing, is currently 50.

A groups profile shows you an overview of the group, date of creation, type of group, how many members, if it has sub groups, the owner of the group and its website. You can look at your groups, search for groups, create your own group and read through LinkedIn's FAQ (Frequently Asked Questions).

LinkedIn Associations allow business professionals to join associations as group members. These associations are usually industry specific. As with all groups, they share content, find answers, post and view jobs and make business connections. Associations provide the ability to attend meetings to meet people on a personal level.

Groups and associations allow you to share your subject matter expertise with like-minded professionals. Those that post interesting content become established authors and often gain industry followers, enhancing their social value.

From a job seeker perspective, there are several good reasons to join a group or association:

1. **You can target specific companies** – learn more about people who work at a specific targeted companies that you would like to work for and learn more about what they do.
2. **Personal Interest** – You can learn more about an industry, product or find companies in that industry.
3. **Professional Association** – Connect with others in a specific association and learn more about jobs or people that are part of the same.
4. **Establish Credibility** – By posting interesting, relevant content about an industry, product or related topic, others will follow you to establish your credibility as an subject matter professional.

LinkedIn also allows you to *start your own group* to share content, find answers, share job openings, make business contacts, etc.

How to Utilize LinkedIn in Your Job Search

Now that we've covered the fundamentals of LinkedIn, we'll explore some advanced techniques to utilize it as it relates to job search. Here again, while I can make suggestions and provide general guidance, it would be futile to provide step by step instructions since LinkedIn regularly changes its pages, navigation and services.

However, it is important to track and record your LinkedIn goals in a "To Do Check List". This will help you reach the target numbers of connections, groups, recommendations, etc. to assist you in building a complete profile.

LinkedIn to Do List

Activity List	Count	Completion
Connections (1st Degree)	>500	☐
Groups & Associations	30 - 50	☐
Target Company List	30 - 50	☐
Recommendations	4 - 7	☐
Skills & Experience (Ask for Endorsements)		☐
URL – Customized to full name (www.linkedIn.com/in/yourname)		☐

Figure 9-2: LinkedIn to Do List

Job Postings

It's one thing to search job boards and another to utilize LinkedIn's Job search feature. Many job boards only post by title and location. The problem is that while you may be seeking a Marketing Manager position, you may be searching in the medical device industry. The job board posting may be a Marketing Manager in the oil and gas industry which is not where you are looking. Valuable time can be wasted on job boards only to realize you're not a fit.

Currently, LinkedIn has a "Jobs" link where you can search for jobs or companies. Without paying for a premium service, you can search for types of jobs and by location. However, with LinkedIn's paid subscription, you can use the advanced job search to include detailed criteria. The advanced search feature allows you to locate positions in specific companies and/or locations that fit your personal marketing plan.

LinkedIn's Advanced Search Functions

One of the best features of LinkedIn paid services is the ability to conduct research. While most people post their profile on LinkedIn and leave it, savvy LinkedIn users take advantage of LinkedIn's ability to learn about jobs, companies, research individuals, study competitors and even market their companies.

Learn about Companies and Hiring Managers

Many companies post their profiles in the same way that individuals do. This information includes the products and services they provide, their company culture and core values as well as information about the company's financial information.

During a job search, LinkedIn allows you to find current and former employees at a specific company. LinkedIn will let you know where you have connections to individuals in your network. For example, when there's a job posting, you may be able to locate someone in your network that knows who the hiring manager is or is someway connected to the company.

Researching and communicating with these individuals can provide you with key intelligence that can give you an edge over other candidates seeking the same position. These contacts may provide personal insight on a potential boss, what skills the company is looking for, what the company culture is really like and much more.

Getting an introduction to a hiring manager through one of your contacts also provides a key networking opportunity. Personal introductions increase your chances of getting a much closer look from a hiring manager.

During your search, you can use LinkedIn to learn a great deal about a hiring manager by reviewing his or her personal business profile. You may want to search for commonalties such as professional associations, mutual acquaintances, educational background, sports, common interests, hobbies, etc. Knowing where the interviewer went to school or referencing common acquaintances, can provide you with good subject matter for a casual conversation, personal correspondence or for an upcoming interview. This information can help to catapult you to the top of the pack by making a strong personal connection with them.

Create Followers to Improve Your Job Search

Like Facebook and other forms of social media, LinkedIn provides a platform to generate content and create "followers", who recognize someone's expertise in specific subject matter. Those who create on-line content are far more likely to get noticed than those that don't. This will ultimately create higher ranking in on-line searches. In social media, this content generation is commonly referred to as "Blogging" (a truncation of the expression known as web logs). Blogging is a posting of relevant information which in-turn, creates an on-line discussion with responses from others.

In LinkedIn, this is especially common when you are part of groups and associations. Unlike Facebook which has discussions on social and political issues, LinkedIn blogs typically provide commentary on business related subjects or specific industry topics. These blogs may combine images with text, provide links to other blogs, web pages or other media. The ability of readers to leave comments in an interactive format is what is important to the contributing author's popularity.

Social Media Involvement

To build followers in social media, you need to get involved in the online community. Many LinkedIn users are content with just having an online profile while others choose to build social connections by being content generators. Of course, celebrities bypass all the rules and have lots of followers, simply because they are popular and people want to hear what they have to say. Business leaders like Warren Buffet, Jeff Bezos or Bill Gates can get legions of followers just by putting their name on something.

For the rest of us, in order to build followers, we need to participate in social media discussions. I have provided a chart below to show the hierarchy of social media involvement and how it affects your online presence.

Levels of Social Media Involvement

INACTIVE
Avoids:
• Does Nothing

VIEWER
Views:
• Reads Blogs
• Watches Videos

JOINER
Updates:
• Profiles
• Joins Groups
• Reads

CRITIC
Writes:
• Reviews
• Posts
• Replies
• Responses

CREATOR
Creates:
• Blogs
• Podcasts
• Videos
• Content

Critical to effective Social Networking

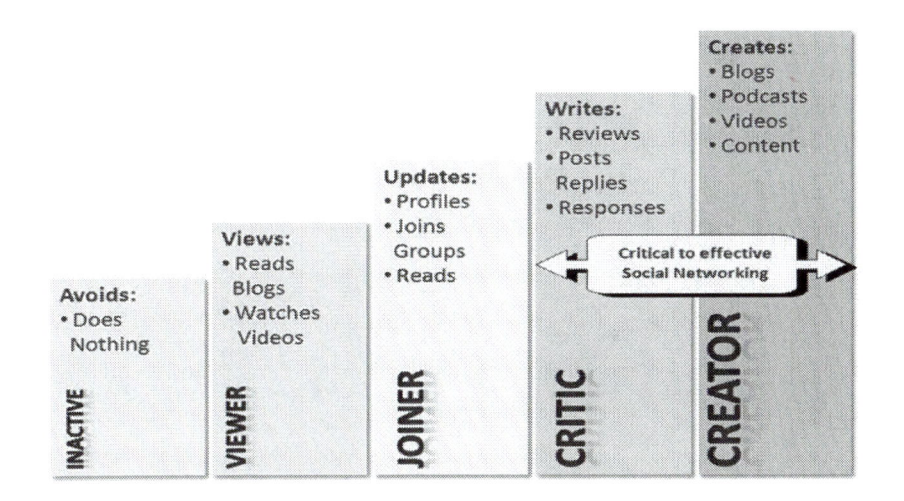

Figure 9- 3: Social Media Involvement

Social media involvement can be shown in 5 categories:

- **Inactive** – Many LinkedIn users do not understand what social networking is or what it can do for them. This type of LinkedIn user creates a profile then leaves it alone just sitting online. The longer their profile remains inactive, the less the chance their profile will appear in a search. They simply get left behind.

- **Viewer** – a viewer reads on-line content and/or watches videos but not much else. Typically, they are not actively involved with groups or associations.

- **Joiner** – a joiner is a common category of social media users. Joiners typically have a Facebook, LinkedIn, Twitter, and other social media accounts. They are similar to viewers but they often join groups and associations, reading their content.

- **Critic** – a critic isn't necessarily a content author but will write reviews and comment on social media posts. Critics will challenge authors on subject matter as well as agree or disagree with content in posts. If you want to be an effective social networker, you'll need to be at minimum, involved as a critic.

- **Creator** – This is the top level of involvement in social media. A creator is just what its title says. It is someone who authors social media content through blogs, podcasts or videos. Creators become social media authorities as they collect more and more followers. Right or not, followers become believers and authors become recognized.

Being a Content Creator Can Shorten Your Job Search

Social media creators help themselves in their job search. Since LinkedIn is the predominant social media site for business, it is ideal for creating content and gaining followers. As an example, let's say that your experience is in marketing. You regularly post articles, tips and suggestions on how to acquire new customers using on-line marketing, how to measure the effectiveness of your website using analytics, etc. etc. People tell others about your posts and before long you become known as a marketing expert. More and more people begin to follow your posts. As you gain more followers, recruiters and / or employers looking to fill a marketing position will find it easier to locate you because they or someone you are connected to considers you to have strong marketing expertise.

The same applies to becoming a member of a group or association. By regularly posting your articles and suggestions (assuming you are contributing content that is valuable to the other members), others will recognize your expertise on the related subject matter. When others believe you have valuable knowledge and expertise in certain subject matter, they will forward job openings and, in some cases, even recommend you.

Targeting Companies

LinkedIn provides the capability to "target" specific companies in your job search. "Targeting Companies" is a different approach to the traditional job search methodology. Locating a job posting and applying along with dozens if not hundreds of other candidates, is not the most effective way to land a position. Using the targeting companies approach, you research the companies that you would like to work for and introduce yourself to potential hiring managers. We will discuss this targeting companies' methodology in the next chapter.

Alternatives to LinkedIn - Searching for Jobs On-line

In addition to LinkedIn, most candidates will typically search for jobs through Google, Yahoo, Bing and other search engines. This is not to be discounted as more and more employers are using the web to locate good candidates at a fraction of the cost of a retained search. While statistics show that about 1/3 or 34% of jobs are actually acquired through an on-line postings, do not completely ignore the power of the internet in a job search. More than 80% of candidates do use the internet to search for information on jobs. The important point is to spend a percentage of your time online, balancing it with your other key activities such as networking.

Job Boards

There are many job boards available on the Internet (Careerbuilder.com, Indeed.com, Theladders.com, Twitter jobs, Google jobs, Craigslist.com, Simplyhired.com, Monster.com, 6figurejobs.com, ritesite.com, jobfox.com, netshare.com, etc.), and as with anything, some are better than others. Most of these sites are paid for by the employers posting the job. As with websites in general, the new model for job boards is moving toward free BASIC level capabilities and higher level functionality at a premium.

There are some job boards that only operate with a paid membership. These are typically geared toward executive level positions such as www.execunet.com. Their model is simple, the job seeker pays and the employers search for free. Since all job sites are in it to make money, expect to see more multi-level job sites with free basic and paid features.

You can also find specific industry job boards such as (Technology Related) dice.com, techcareers.com, etc. or (Healthcare Related) medzilla.com, HealthJobsUSA.com, allhealthjobs.com. Do a simple Google search for key words such as "medical jobs", etc. and you will find many sites.

Here are a few suggestions in using Job Boards:

- ❒ Take the time to list your resume on the job boards so you can receive maximum exposure from any potential employers. (Resume blasters are a waste of money)

- ❒ Each time you visit the job board site BE SURE TO MODIFY AND REACTIVATE YOUR RESUME. This action moves your resume to the top of the search trees (Most recently placed resumes are viewed first by employers).

- When you respond to a potential opportunity, make sure you meet the general criteria. These sites receive so many resumes, they will not even respond, and you will be wasting your valuable time.

- If possible, call the potential employer. We discuss what to say in greater detail in the Targeting Companies chapter. Personal contact is always helpful in selling yourself.

Step 3

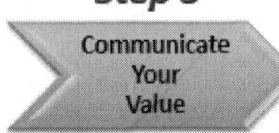

Communicate Your Value

Learn To "Target" Companies

Chapter 10

TARGETING COMPANIES

This chapter applies most all of what we've discussed in this book about job search and is probably the most important one we'll cover. The Targeting Companies method is today's approach to locating professional employment and reducing wasted efforts in applying. Targeting companies is an approach to selectively *target* the companies you want to work for and network your way into a position.

Did you ever notice that most companies prefer to hire from within before going outside the company? The reason is that most employers are more comfortable knowing that the employees that apply are *known entities*. It is only when employers don't feel they have the right talent internally that they choose to go outside.

Targeting companies can effectively create the same result for you. When you are a potential candidate, you can become a known entity through networking. By making connections with potential employers before they post jobs will increase your potential of getting hired.

The "Targeting Companies" Approach

Targeting companies is a job search approach that starts with making a list of companies you would like to work for, finding the names of people that could potentially hire you and connecting with them through networking. This approach will help you find a career that aligns with your personal skills, passions, culture, values and abilities to impact the company's goals and needs.

Using the targeting companies' process, you can potentially seek out opportunities <u>before</u> they get posted to the public. By meeting / networking with a potential hiring manager before a job gets posted, you gain the opportunity to impress them enough to make you an offer. The fact is, once a job is posted, there are hundreds of job seekers that apply and the employer has many candidates to choose from. The idea is to avoid this rush of other job seekers who end up competing for the same position.

The Old Rules of Job Search

Many job seekers go straight to the internet, look on job boards and send their resume/application into cyber space, thinking that they will get a call back for an interview. Here is a reality check. Few candidates ever receive a non-automated response let alone a chance to interview. In most cases, your resume goes into the black hole of the employers ATS database and you'll probably never hear from them again.

Other candidates try, what I call "non-purposed networking". They meet with other unemployed people over coffee and get few if any results. Some hand out resumes to everyone they come in contact with. Most those resumes end up in the trash can as soon as you leave.

The New Rules of Job Search

As we've discussed, the internet and social media are continuing to change how we search for a job. Because of this, the sheer volume of applicants for any one online job posting has forced employers to change the way they collect, review and store applicant information. This is the reason the old rules no longer apply.

Finding and landing a position today requires a "targeted" strategy. That is, don't send resumes to every job opening you can find. Instead, use a targeted networking and social media (LinkedIn) approach to locate positions and meet people that can make the right introductions. It's all about packaging and selling your value to people that are connected to the company or industry you are "targeting".

The internet has also given employers the ability to find you instead of the other way around. As we discussed in the previous chapter, make yourself visible online with a strong LinkedIn profile. Make sure your messaging communicates your potential value as an employee.

However, targeting companies is NOT simply making a list of companies that you would like to work for and sending off your resume to each one. If you only make a list and send resumes out, your resume will most likely end up in HR (Human Resources). Once that occurs, it will follow the HR process of ensuring that you meet ALL the criteria. The important part of the targeting companies process is contacting and communicating with <u>potential hiring managers</u>.

Here is an overview of how the Targeting Companies process works:

The Targeting Companies Process

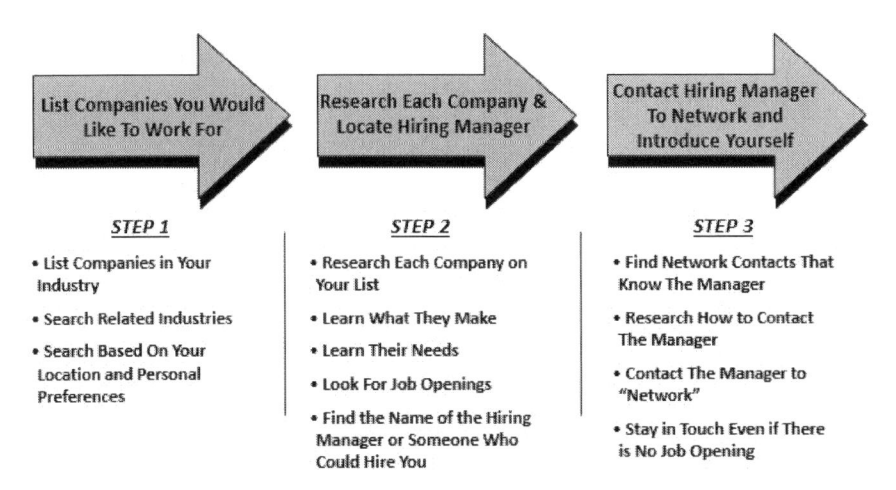

STEP 1 — List Companies You Would Like To Work For
- List Companies in Your Industry
- Search Related Industries
- Search Based On Your Location and Personal Preferences

STEP 2 — Research Each Company & Locate Hiring Manager
- Research Each Company on Your List
- Learn What They Make
- Learn Their Needs
- Look For Job Openings
- Find the Name of the Hiring Manager or Someone Who Could Hire You

STEP 3 — Contact Hiring Manager To Network and Introduce Yourself
- Find Network Contacts That Know The Manager
- Research How to Contact The Manager
- Contact The Manager to "Network"
- Stay in Touch Even if There is No Job Opening

Figure 10-1: The Targeting Companies Process

The reason targeting companies is effective is that it does not follow the traditional process of locating a job opening and filing out an employment application. By speaking directly to hiring managers, you'll have the opportunity to present your functional knowledge about the subject matter that is important to that individual.

When you send a resume or fill out a job application, the only information the employer sees has about you is a written, chronological history of where you've worked. The advantage of using the targeting companies approach is that it provides you with an opportunity to sell your value directly to a hiring manager rather than sending your resume to human resources. Unless you've worked for a competitor, a resume will not convey as much about your real skills and value that a conversation with the hiring manager will. Here is a real life example:

Bob's Story

Bob had recently worked as the head of service at a large BMW dealership, reporting directly to the General Manager. After 18 years of service, he was called into his bosses office and told that the dealership was letting him go. Despite the fact that Bob's service revenue numbers were exceptional and customer satisfaction was at an all-time high, Bob could not comprehend why they would ever consider letting him go.

The fact is, many times senior managers and business owners feel they need to make changes to further improve business. When things continue to work well for long periods of time and great results appear to be the "norm", it's easy to become complacent. Unfortunately, without day to day hands on knowledge, some managers really don't know how effective their team is and believe that by making changes, they can improve.

More often than not, this scenario plays out all over corporate America. It usually doesn't work out well for the business after the changes are made, and you rarely hear about it because no one ever wants to admit they made a mistake!

Bob was very upset as his world became unbalanced. Without much thought, he decided to make a career change. Tired of all the problems that a GM faces daily, life could be easier if he became a lower level service writer. Even though his paycheck would be cut in half, he felt that he should work as an individual contributor, reduce his stress level and accept a new reality.

He began his search by driving around town to other dealerships leaving resumes and filling out applications. Unfortunately, nothing seemed to pan out. What he failed to realize was the emotional grief he was going through was affecting the way he interacted with potential employers (we discussed this in Chapter 2).

Bob was in a panic and called me to explain his situation. I suggested to Bob that he needed to stop everything he was doing and get his emotions in check before continuing any type of job search activity! To make my point clear, I reminded him that there are a finite number of dealerships in the area and he could easily exhaust the supply of potential employers. This was especially important to him, considering he did not want to relocate his family.

I suggested that Bob take a different approach to his job search, using the targeting companies method. Since Bob already had extensive experience as a senior service manager, he must know other General Managers and dealership owners in the area.

Bob made a target company list of all the dealerships he had senior level contacts with. He began calling them to reconnect and told them he was seeking new opportunities.

Within 2 weeks, Bob received a call from one of the dealership owners who asked if he could help with a project. The owner wanted to tap Bob's expertise to evaluate and recommend service test equipment to upgrade his dealerships' diagnostic systems.

By working closely with the owner on the project, Bob impressed him with his knowledge of automotive service systems and processes. Within a month, Bob was offered and accepted the top Service Manager position at one of the owners other dealerships!

Why the Targeting Companies Approach is Effective

A 2017 study conducted by Western University and published in the *Journal of Experimental Social Psychology* had 45 participants ask 450 strangers (10 strangers each) to complete a brief survey. All the participants made the exact same request following the exact same script; however, half of the participants made their requests over email, while the other half asked face-to-face. Those who made their requests face-to-face were *34 times* more effective than emailed ones!

The Western University study demonstrated a significant difference in human behavior responses, comparing face-to-face requests versus email. It validates why the targeting companies approach of speaking directly with a hiring manager provides a better chance of success than sending an emailed resume does.

The following provides a step by step approach to target companies.

Step 1 - Define Your Job Search Criteria

In order to begin using the targeting companies approach, we need to go back to our chapter 4 discussion about making career direction decisions. As part of the process, we are revisiting the following criterion to make a final decision for each. Your responses to each one directly affect what companies you should select for your target company list.

- ❐ **How far are you willing to commute to a job every day?** You'll want to select companies in your target list that fall within your travel time comfort zone. If you are willing to commute over an hour each way every day, go for it but be realistic. I have seen candidates accept jobs that are over 2 hours commute each way just because they felt the need to generate an income. This includes those commuting to different cities and living away during the week. This length of commute is difficult to sustain on a long-term basis as it cuts deeply into your personal and family time. Think carefully about this. Only you can answer for you but most importantly, be honest with yourself.

☐ **Are you willing to relocate?** Aside from commute time, would you seriously consider relocating? If the answer is yes, you need to be fully committed to move, understand the costs involved and have your family / spouse / partner in agreement. Relocating requires breaking emotional ties with family and friends and can wreak havoc on children, especially those at certain ages. This also means that you may want to consider targeting the type of companies that would pay for your relocation. In today's business climate, fewer companies are willing to shell out the big relocation bucks unless you are applying at a high enough level in the organization. You must consider all of the relocation costs as you may end up paying all or some of them.

Relocations can get very expensive so research and evaluate all the costs involved before moving forward. A household move across the county can cost upwards of $20,000! These costs may involve selling and buying a home including commissions / closing costs, relocating all your furniture and belongings, travel expenses, temporary lodging and other costs. If you are looking to purchase a home in a new area, you'll need to determine if it's financially feasible due to differences in the cost of living. In high priced markets such as New York City, San Francisco or Los Angeles, you may find that renting may be your only option. If you are considering relocation, do your homework before you commit!

☐ **What geographical areas are you willing to locate to?** If you answered "yes" to relocating, how far away are you willing to move. Are there any specific areas you are _not_ willing to move to? For example, if you grew up and live in the heat of south Florida, you may find it difficult to move to cold weather cities like Chicago or Minneapolis and adjust to the frigid winter climate.

Would you consider a position in another country? In addition to the positions in the USA, there are opportunities in Canada, the U.K., Australia, Europe, Singapore, Japan, China, Hong Kong, India, South America, Africa, the Middle East as well as other countries. There are far more open positions available on a worldwide basis if you are willing to relocate. Depending where you move, you may find living overseas very different both financially and culturally. Many things that you are used to having or doing may not be available. If you decide that you are willing to locate anywhere, do your homework and decide which countries you want to target.

☐ **What size company do you want to work for?** Different size companies have different cultural personalities. Working for a large fortune 500 company is quite different than working for a small, 25-person "mom and pop" company. Some find the change difficult, moving from one size company to another.

Large corporations are process oriented, resource rich and limit your scope to specific targets and objectives. Small and start-up companies are just the opposite. There are very few resources and employees are required to handle many different roles or tasks. There are typically little, if any, formal processes in small companies. Make sure you understand and are willing to accept the size of the company you want to work for before you move forward.

- **What industry do you want to work in?** Many people believe it is impossible to change industries. The truth is, it is more difficult but it is possible. Ask yourself, do you want to stay in your current industry? If your answer is yes, make sure you do the research on your current industry to ensure its future viability.

  As an example of this, cameras have become an integrated part in almost all cell phones. For camera manufacturers, the number of jobs in that specific industry has decreased. If you happened to be someone in the camera manufacturing industry, it would probably be wise to consider making a change. Your skills may be very transferable to other industries as well as the companies that integrate cameras into their phones. Remember, finance is finance, engineering is engineering, etc. If you're considering changing industries, target companies that can use your related skills.

- **What kind of salary do you need to sustain your lifestyle?** Do the math and make sure you understand the minimum salary you need to pay your bills. We covered this financial exercise earlier in Chapter 3. Knowing what your fixed and discretionary expenses are each month will help you determine the salary you will need to make at a minimum. Consider other compensation options such as paid health care, bonuses, equity, company car, cell phone expenses, etc. as these may substitute for some compromises in salary.

- **What job title are you looking for?** This doesn't sound like much of a consideration and it is probably not, but be realistic. Obtaining a job with a similar level title is more likely to happen than obtaining one at a higher level. However, moving from a large company to a smaller one can certainly impact your title.

For example, a director level manager at a large corporation could have had 300 or 400 employees in his or her organization. Moving to a small company, this candidate could likely receive a Vice President title. I suggest you focus on getting the job you want, not the title.

Step 2 - Create Your Personal Target Company List

Once you've answered the questions and determined what your needs are, you'll need to create a target list of companies which meet your same criteria.

1) Make a list of the companies you would ideally like to work for. Create a list with a minimum of 25-50 companies. You can go larger, but keep the list to a maximum of 100 companies to ensure it is manageable. One of the easiest tools to help you find and create your target list is LinkedIn. LinkedIn provides the ability to

search for companies by name or keyword. You can also search for companies by location, industry or by company size.

2) Prioritize your list of companies with the one's you would most like to work for at the top. Don't prioritize them by their brand. Rank them by how well they fit your criteria for company size, commute time, benefits, geography, etc. LinkedIn's search criteria also provide you with the ability to enter a company name or keyword such as "construction" or "medical device". Company searches can be limited to only those that currently have job postings. It also provides the ability to find other types of companies by browsing related industries. This will help you determine if each company should or should not remain on your list.

3) While you are creating your list in your current industry, consider related industries. Find companies in those industries that could utilize your career skills. Targeting companies is not only an effective method to locate hidden job opportunities but can also be effective in transitioning industries. Despite what you perceive, you <u>can</u> change industries and people do it all the time. Changing industries is certainly more difficult, but it is not impossible.

Consider this, if you are in finance, a balance sheet, profit and loss statement, and other types of financial statements are similar if not identical, regardless of industry. Electrical engineering is still electrical engineering regardless of industry. While products, markets and processes may be different, many of the core skills are the same, regardless of industry. The most difficult transitions are for sales and marketing people as their expertise is typically tied to an industry. However, selling principles are the same regardless of industry or product.

Research shows that 10 to 15% of those changing jobs enter a new industry or field. Research also shows an average employee will change jobs 7 to 10 times during their career, some moving to a completely different type of business.

Step 3 – Research Each Company

Once you have compiled your target list of companies, you'll need to conduct some additional research. Search for detailed information about each company on your target list, starting with the companies of highest preference. In addition to using LinkedIn, search each target company's website. Your research can help you learn whether or not you can add value. The key is to dig in and gain as much knowledge about each company as you can.

- ❐ Check LinkedIn and websites for each of your target company's for job openings. Is there an open position requisition that fits your background and skill set? Job postings are typically found under the headers of "careers" or "employment". They may also be found in a sub-menu under "Contact Us" or "About Us". Use your personal criteria to search jobs in different locations if relocation is something you are willing to consider. The good news is you may find your target company already has an open position where you may be a fit. The downside of this is that you now have a number of candidates to compete with.

  You can also search job boards such as Indeed, Monster, CareerBuilder, ZipRecruiter, Craigslist, Ladders, Dice, etc. to locate openings at companies on your targeted list. If you find the target company does not show an open position that you fit, don't let it deter you. Nearly every employer is interested in locating top talent, regardless of whether or not they have a job opening. Believe it or not, companies will create positions if they come across someone they believe is talented and is a good cultural fit.

☐ Learn what each company makes or the type of services they provide. Your understanding of each company's products and/or services will not only help to decide whether you are a good fit but will also help you to have knowledgeable discussions with people inside the company.

☐ During your research, locate the names of people you know that either work at the target company or that may know someone who works at the target company. LinkedIn is especially good at this in searches. There is always a possibility that you may not know anyone, but you need to go through the process for each company you target. The goal is to find the name and title of a person that works in a department that could potentially hire you, even if they don't have an open position.

☐ While you are looking, try to learn what the company culture is like (e.g. team focused, top down, etc.)? Company culture is a very important piece of the puzzle. It should match your own personal criteria. For example, some companies operate in intense "pressure cooker" environments while others have a more casual, relaxed atmosphere. You need to know something about each company's culture to change their rank on your list.

- ☐ Search the "media" section of each company's website to gain valuable insight from the company's news releases. Through this, you can explore relevant information such as expansion news, store openings, organizational change announcements, expansion plans, acquisitions, etc. Any time there is growth or change, it typically translates into the need for more talent. "Organizational changes" usually signal that people will be leaving and potentially create new opportunities for you.

- ☐ It's also a good idea to research each company's financial statements, annual reports, etc. In addition to searching the company's website, use Google finance, Google news, Yahoo finance, Morningstar.com or other financial websites to look for financial information about the company. This information will tell you about the company's financial health and will help determine if they should move higher or lower on your list. For example, if the company's financial outlook is weak or modest, you should recognize that it will be more difficult to get hired. After learning this, it may be wise to scratch them off your target company list.

- ☐ What other industries or related positions could you contribute to? Don't box yourself into looking for the same job in the same industry. There are other potential opportunities out there for you, providing you do the research.

Additional Information Target Companies Sources

Other sources of information for researching these companies are available in your local library. Public libraries offer many sources on the very companies you are looking to target. Libraries have access to on-line data base services such as Dunn & Bradstreet, Hoovers, etc. They often have a selection of magazine subscriptions including trade publications, standard register books and local business publications such as business journals

Joining job or industry specific groups can help you locate contacts and jobs that are not posted or advertised. These groups include IT, medical device, financial, marketing and many other disciplines.

Step 4 - Locate a Potential Hiring Manager

Now that you have a list of companies to target and you've researched information about each company, you'll need to locate a manager/supervisor/executive in the company that could hire someone like you. Think about what their title would be.

If you are a VP of Marketing, you are most likely to be hired by the President /CEO so you would target the President /CEO. If you are a Director of Marketing, you might be hired by the VP of Marketing, so you would target the VP/CMO (Chief Marketing Officer) and so on down the line of reporting.

What were the titles of the last positions you held? Chances are the titles you are looking for are similar. In any case, follow the hierarchy of an organization to see where your position fits.

Once you have decided the title or titles of managers that could potentially hire, you will need to locate the name of the person that currently holds that position at each target company. Start by using LinkedIn, each company's website and internet searches. There are a variety of search tools that can help.

- **Use LinkedIn, Facebook, Twitter and other social media sites** to profile the companies. Many companies today have a large presence in social media and this trend continues to grow even to small companies. Conduct a search to find people in your network who might know someone at each target company. When you have a LinkedIn profile, you can see how many people pop up who are former colleagues or friends from your past.

- **Use a Google, Yahoo or Bing search** using the title and the name of the company as the keyword. Use phrases such as "VP Marketing Allergan". Keep in mind, the higher the position level; the easier it is to locate the target person. A CMO or CEO's name is typically in the news releases or public company reports. Obviously the larger the company, the more challenging it will be to locate lower level names.

- **Use people finder internet sites** such as Lead411.com, zoominfo.com and Hoovers.com to locate people. Although some of these type of search sites require a paid subscription, check with your local library to see if they already have a subscription available for public use.

- **Call the company on the telephone** and ask for the name of the person with that title. Some companies will provide names and others will not. Companies are always interested in doing business but are less likely to divulge names to job seekers so be creative in the way you ask. You can be resourceful and still be honest.

- **Use networking to re-establish connections with people from your past.** Create a list of names of friends, acquaintances, former colleagues, trade associations, personal groups, and relatives. LinkedIn is very useful as a tool to make contact and reconnect as it not only provides information on their whereabouts, but offers a method of social media communication. Send your contacts a "catch-up" note and invite them to reconnect. Let them know that you are seeking a new career opportunity and ask them for specific contacts at target companies. Don't forget to ask how you can help them and try to stay in touch.

Step 5 – Meet with the Hiring Manager

The strategy behind targeting companies is simple, the more meetings you can get with company managers, the greater the number of chances you will get to impress someone enough to offer you an opportunity or <u>even create a job for you</u>! The key is to communicate your value as it relates to the needs of each targeted company.

During my own job transition, I personally targeted medical device companies. Through a network contact, I managed to get a meeting with the President of one of the company's divisions. From that meeting, he was impressed enough to create a new position for me and offered me an opportunity to become the new Vice President of Marketing. How much competition did I have for the job? Zero! The job was never posted!

Target your way to your next job!

The lesson here is simple. The probability of landing is far less if you're job search strategy is sitting in front of a computer applying for jobs on job sites. Instead, focus your efforts on creating opportunities to meet with potential employers. Employers are always looking for the right people that can solve problems and fit into their corporate culture. Keep working at it!

Step 3
Communicate Your Value

Network Your Way Into A Job

Chapter 11

GET OUT THERE AND NETWORK!

Let's face it, the only constant in today's business world is change! Regardless of what job, industry or level of position you have held, career transition is an integral part of Corporate America. According to surveys, the average position lasts between 18 and 36 months, depending on the type of company and industry you are in.

If you are currently working and are looking to make a change, or have become unemployed, networking is by far the most effective way to land a position. Consider this; according to a 2018 survey by Performance-Based Hiring Learning Systems, 85% of respondents found their job via networking! Based on these kind of statistics, networking is key to the on-going process of Career Life Cycle Management!

What is "Networking"

When you're looking for a job, you've probably heard this a hundred times;

"the best way to locate a position is through networking". The problem is many people don't understand what "networking" really means.

Networking is NOT sending out e-mail blasts to everyone you know. It is not meeting with people and asking them for a job. Exchanging business cards is not networking nor is having coffee with everyone without a purpose.

Networking is a process in which you look for opportunities to meet people to begin relationship building activities. It is establishing connections with others and not just meeting them, but <u>building on-going relationships</u> with them. This means joining groups and organizations, volunteering together, worshiping together and meeting regularly. The stronger the relationship, the higher the probability you will receive a referral or possibly a recommendation.

I'm sure you would agree that a hiring manager is more likely to pay attention to a résumé or recommendation received from someone they know and trust. Think about this. The fear of selecting the wrong candidate always weighs heavily on hiring managers. A bad hiring decision can be costly to a managers personal career!

Part of every manager's performance evaluation criteria is the ability to hire and retain quality candidates. Managers fear the consequences of making bad hiring decisions and will almost always go with the safest candidate choice. Network recommendations can be very helpful in a job search.

It's Who You Know

We learned early in life about the value of networking. Having said that, we may not have thought of networking in the same context as we do during a job search. Most people have some experience or have seen the benefits of knowing a policeman, a teacher or a politician who helped them or someone they knew. Through network connections, people receive free tickets, get invited to special events, receive discounts, get freebies and the list goes on. We never called it "networking" but we've likely seen the benefits of knowing people in positions of authority.

Networking Applies Everywhere

While you are attending cocktail or dinner party, wedding, sporting event, etc. why not strike up a conversation with the person right next to you? They could be the person that introduces you to your next job! No matter how smart or talented you believe you are, you will not have the same competitive edge as someone who is well connected.

There is a well-known adage you have probably heard; ***"It's not what you know, but who you know"***. This is especially true during the job search process. Only when people know you and you get to know them will they help you.

By developing relationships, networking will help you advance your professional (and maybe social) life. It will best serve you if you remember that networking is sharing. It's a give and take that benefits all parties.

When you network with others, you gain valuable insights about yourself, gather information about opportunities and build positive relationships. This applies everywhere as connections can be made in some of the most unlikely places. Here is one of them:

Rick's Story

Rick had been searching for an operations management position. To get out of the house, Rick went on a daily trek to the local Starbucks for coffee. Every morning he'd see Brenda, who would greet him with a smile and take his coffee order.

As the weeks passed, Brenda and Rick got to know each other better, moving past the morning greeting onto more substantive conversation. One of the benefits of networking is to reach a point where both people feel comfortable enough to discuss more personalized information.

Brenda told Rick that she was about to begin her first year of college in the fall and was very excited. Rick explained that he was unemployed and was searching for an operations management position, particularly in a medical device company.

Brenda mentioned that her father was the CEO of a medical device company and offered to make an introduction. After meeting Brenda's father, Rick received an opportunity he never expected. A connection made through a college student working at Starbucks, turned into a new job for Rick!

The point here is that network connections can come from anyone and anywhere. You never know where your next job connection will be made or with whom, so take advantage of every opportunity to network with others!

Levels of Networking

Networking doesn't happen instantly. Just because you met someone for a cup of coffee doesn't mean you have built a relationship. Relationships must be cultivated over time. In the previous Starbucks story, Rick spent months going to the same Starbucks where he eventually got to know the woman that made the connection for him.

There are various stages of networking based upon the level of knowledge, trust and respect between people. Networking is built on first establishing these types of relationships and then staying in contact. If you begin to network only when you need something, you will find you have a lot of catching up to do. Instead of waiting until you're unemployed or need help from someone, stay involved in some form of regular networking.

The following graphic represents the levels of networking relationships:

Levels of Networking

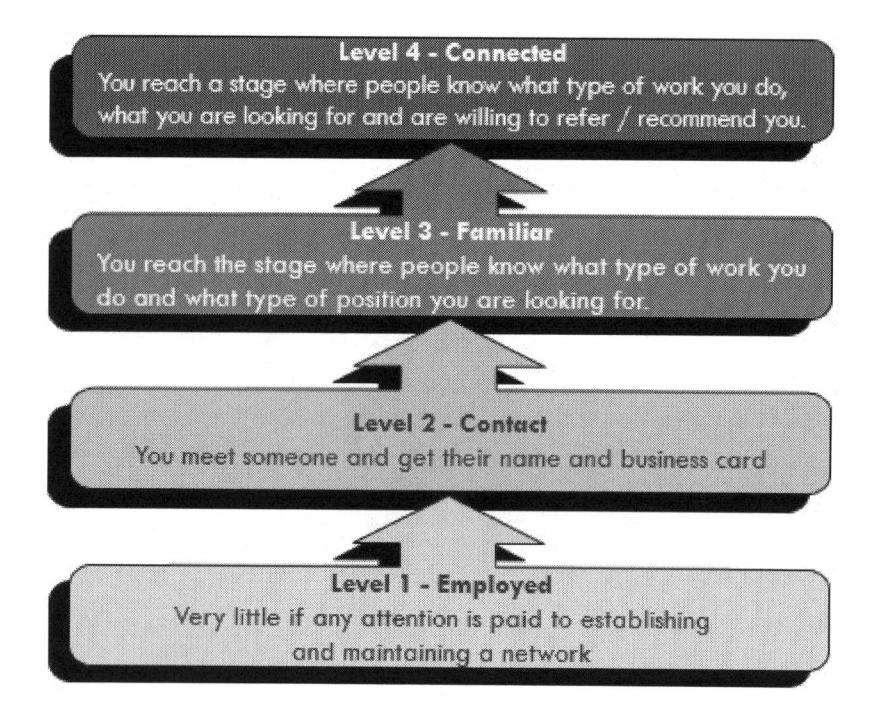

Level 4 - Connected
You reach a stage where people know what type of work you do, what you are looking for and are willing to refer / recommend you.

Level 3 - Familiar
You reach the stage where people know what type of work you do and what type of position you are looking for.

Level 2 - Contact
You meet someone and get their name and business card

Level 1 - Employed
Very little if any attention is paid to establishing and maintaining a network

Figure 11-1: Levels of Networking

Level 1 - Employed - A common mistake made by employed people is maintaining a false sense of job security. The truth is, no job is secure. This fallacy makes it easy to convince yourself that you are just too busy to network.

While you are employed, it is a good idea to network with people in own workplace. Don't skip going out on impromptu celebrations or bypass the Christmas party just because you are uncomfortable around company social events and your co-workers. For many people making social contact is work and it is easier just to go home.

Wherever there is an opportunity to network, take advantage of it and engage. When your co-workers feel your personal connection and appreciate what you do, they will be more likely to help safeguard your position during uncertain times.

While you are employed, you should consider your current job as a "temporary employment assignment". It is part of an on-going career life management strategy which will most likely change. Few people stay in the same position for their entire career. In fact, statistics show that the average position lasts up to a mere 36 months with management positions even less at 24 -30 months.

Networking is important, so don't avoid it, just because you are not comfortable reaching out to others. Network contacts can lead you to various opportunities that one day may enhance or change your career. You can stay networked by attending business and social meetings as well as joining clubs, groups and associations. Active participation in community and professional organizations will also help you stay known to others.

Don't expect instant results if you start networking the day you need a job. At minimum, staying connected will shorten the time it takes to find your next career assignment when you want or need to.

Level 2 - Contact - When you meet someone and get their name or business card, it is a good place to start networking. Consider it an introduction. You don't really know that person and they don't know you.

After collecting a pile of business cards at a network function, it is challenging to remember who each person was that you met the previous day.

Immediately after receiving someone's card, write down information you took away from the conversation and follow-up with them. They will be impressed that you took the initiative and are likely to meet with you again. At minimum, send them an invitation to join your LinkedIn network.

Future meetings with these same individuals become the basis for developing relationships. You want others get to know who you are and what you do. Never forget that networking is not just about you. The person you meet with may be in transition or looking for their next job and you could be that someone that can help them.

The network pros will tell you that giving is just as important as receiving. If you have been on the receiving end from someone who has helped you, they become a special person in your life; one that you will always remember and appreciate. The same holds true if you help them.

Level 3 - Familiar – When you regularly attend networking meetings, you often see the same people. While some attend to market their own talents and job skills, most people attend functions to meet other industry professionals. A few even attend to take advantage of free food and drinks. In any case, attending networking events is important for you to build and maintain a professional network. The more familiar you become to others, the more likely they will get to know you.

Regular meetings allow you to develop new friendships and broaden past business only relationships. Utilize peers and colleagues to solicit feedback and advice.

You will also learn to distinguish those that are interested in building real relationships from those networkers that are only "tuned into" themselves on the selfish channel; WIFM (What's in it for Me). Unfortunately, there are people that are only interested in what you can do for them and not the other way around. Once you become familiar enough with someone, you can make the determination to continue building a relationship or move away and focus on others who reciprocate.

Level 4 - Connected – When you reach the stage in a relationship where the other person knows who you really are and you know them, they may be willing to pass along an unsolicited contact names. Few people are willing to recommend someone they don't know well or have not worked with.

After someone gets to know you well, they are more willing to put their own reputation on the line for you. This is what makes a level 4 network connection so important. The more of these people you connect with, the more contacts and leads will come your way. It's simply a numbers game.

How and Where to Network

Now that we understand that there are different levels of networking, we will discuss HOW and WHERE to network. Like anything, to maximize your networking efforts you'll need to prepare. Networking is another form of marketing promotion where the product is you.

Business owners attend meetings, tradeshows and other marketing events to connect with potential customers This means clearly articulating the value they offer and providing information on staying connected. The same type of marketing applies to you.

To prepare to meet business professionals at events and trade or social functions, you need to know what to say when you describe yourself as the product. You need to be able to communicate your value and what you seeking to others.

Good networkers know how to build rapport with the people they meet. They show a genuine interest in the person they are speaking to and are good listeners. We all know someone who was popular in high school, college or in life. Those popular people learned early in life the importance of asking questions and getting others to talk about themselves. Too often, those looking for a something forget that conversing is a two-way street.

Let's face it, a someone you meet at an event doesn't want or need to hear your entire spiel. Instead of overwhelming them with the gory details about why you are looking for a job and all the reasons why you would be a great employee, focus the conversation on exchanging information, advice and contacts. Find out what they know and who they know. You can only learn by asking about them and listening to them. You can't learn anything if you spend your time yakking about yourself.

Keep in mind, someone you meet could become a future employer, business partner or a client. When someone asks, "so what do you do"? Your response should be your positioning statement which defines who you are, what you are looking for and how you add value to a professional relationship.

Create Your Introduction

Start by simply introducing yourself and tell them who you. What's the most interesting or memorable thing you can say about yourself? You'll want to say something that will get the other person want to know more about you. Leverage the skills you've identified and frame them in a way that is meaningful to your target subject.

As we described in the chapter on "Developing Your Personal Brand", a networking event is where your "elevator statement" comes in to use. You should be able to provide a succinct description of who you are, and what you offer. Know and tell your story using example analogies and just enough details to make it come alive. It should be personal, well-rehearsed and memorable, not your life story or a drawn-out soap box speech. Whenever possible, use a "proof point" to demonstrate that you can do or have done what you say you can. Provide a "call to action" to let that person know what you're looking for.

Don't just go out and network without knowing what you are going to say. Create your script then practice your introduction and how you'll deliver it. Test it out by recording yourself on video or with a friendly audience.

Your Personal Brand (Elevator / Positioning Statement)

As we covered in chapter 5 - *"Developing Your Personal Brand"*, all you need to state is your *position/title, industry, what you seek, and a proof point* to validate what you are saying. Here again is an example:

"I am a *quality manager* in *medical device manufacturing* with a *six-sigma black belt certification*. I am looking for a similar position in a *medical device company* based here in *Chicago*." Not much more needs to be said about you.

Here are some other examples:

"I am a social media HR consultant, specializing in LinkedIn, branding and recruitment".

"I am a Marketing Communications manager in the oil and gas industry with over 10 years' experience. I help businesses build and promote lasting brands."

Close the conversation by asking for help! *"Who do you know that ……..?"*

What to Do at Networking Events

Once you have prepared and rehearsed your introduction (elevator or positioning statement), you need to get out there and network. If you are the type of person that is shy or has difficulty approaching people, it's a good idea to stand near the food and drink table at an event or meeting. People gravitate toward food, providing you with the opportunity to say hello and strike up a casual conversation. Ask about them and when they reciprocate, provide them with your personal brand information.

If you are someone who is comfortable walking up to and talking to strangers, scan the room, taking note of the crowd. Recognize the power networkers in the room. These are people who move around the room having short, friendly conversations with a variety of people. Decide which of them you would like to meet. Ask others if they know that person or make a self-introduction. Keep in mind that they also came to network, so don't be shy when it comes to introducing yourself.

Find a reason to strike up a conversation. Ask a question or make an observation. Try to connect with their common interests by telling a short story about one or two things that you like and observe whether the other person seems interested. Try sharing news or make a positive comment. Mention something that you heard at the event or say something positive about the event.

Some of the best-connected people at the event may be the group organizers or facilitators. Given that these events only run for a few hours, take the time to introduce yourself and talk to the organizers sitting at the front. Find out who the group leaders are and tell them about the value you might be able to provide. Stay in contact with them, get involved by contributing to the group and they will remember who you are and may refer others to you.

After attending an event, follow-up with every person you met. At minimum, send them an invitation to LinkedIn or a follow-up "nice to meet you" email within 72 hours of the event. For those individuals that you felt you could eventually have a mutually beneficial connection with, do the same but attach an article, blog or some type of information that might be of value to them.

Business Cards

Once you meet someone, you'll need to provide them with your contact information. The most common method of providing contact information is handing out a professional business card. Prepare for any networking event you plan to attend by bringing at least 25 - 30 business cards with you to hand out.

Avoid the temptation to print detailed information about you on the back of your business cards. Most people don't read the reverse side and it takes away valuable real estate where notes and reminders can be written.

Business cards are a direct reflection of you, so don't make them on your home computer with cheap looking card templates unless you're a graphic artist using thick, professional blanks.

An economical source for making professional looking business cards can be found online at Vistaprint.com. For the same cost of blank homemade business card templates, you can order 250 custom cards which you can design using Vistaprint's pre-design layouts. Unless you are a graphics pro, Vistaprint cards will look far more professional than homemade computer cards. As an alternative to Vistaprint.com, you may want to consider PrintsMadeEasy.com.

When you meet someone, be sure to exchange business cards. This will ensure you have their contact information and they have yours. It's a good idea to carry a pen in your pocket or purse to write notes on business cards.

During a networking event, you may collect a dozen cards and you won't remember everyone you spoke with. Write notes about them on the back of their card that will help you remember specific things about that person. The notes will help you to remember when you are supposed to follow-up or who you need to introduce them to. When you look at the card months later, you'll remember what the discussion was about, especially when you agreed to follow-up for a future coffee or lunch meeting.

Don't Hand Out Resumes to Networking Events!

When you attend a networking event and hand someone your resume, it creates an awkward situation. They most likely don't want it and they certainly don't want to carry it around.

No one wants to offend you by tossing it out in front of you, but they most likely will get rid of it first chance they get. Unless a person specifically asks for a copy of your resume, don't email it to them either. Giving someone your resume won't accomplish much and is a waste of paper. You'll get better results by starting a relationship based on conversation and follow-up.

Networking Venues are Not the Place to ask for a Job

At a networking event saying, "I'm looking for a job" communicates an in-your-face message that the discussion is about to get uncomfortable. It's not that people are cold or insensitive; it's that they know a stereotypical job-hunter won't talk about much else except what they are looking for in their job search.

This drives people away as it they lose track of what to say except "uh-huh" and "sorry to hear that". We all need sympathetic ears and a networking event might seem like the logical place to tell someone about why you are looking, but it's not.

Who to Network With

Networking begins by getting out and meeting with people. There are thousands of network meetings that go on every day in every city across the country.

Start by identifying people that you already know. This approach covers all types of networks including Professional Networks, Community Networks and Individual Networks. Here are some suggestions of who to network with (in alphabetical order, not order of importance):

- ✓ Attorneys
- ✓ Bankers
- ✓ Business Owners
- ✓ Club Members
- ✓ Common Interest Associates
- ✓ Coworkers
- ✓ Faith Based Community Members
- ✓ Former Employers and Coworkers
- ✓ Friends
- ✓ Local Community Leaders
- ✓ Medical Professionals
- ✓ Neighbors
- ✓ Professional Association Members
- ✓ Relatives
- ✓ Salespeople
- ✓ School or College Acquaintances
- ✓ Vendors

We often lose touch with former colleagues, teachers and friends we once knew. While balancing a demanding job and a family, it's difficult to stay in communication with our past. It is unfortunate that we only think about our former connections when we are looking for a new job or need to make a business connection. Even though we haven't stayed in touch, it's always good idea to contact them and reconnect.

Don't limit yourself to just colleagues in your field. You should also network with people you know. These people include neighbors, former teachers, family and friends as the connection you are looking for may be made through someone you already know.

Reconnect with former contacts via social networking (LinkedIn), by e-mail or telephone. Start by asking how and what they are doing and let them reply to you! Once you have reconnected, they will mention how they are and will usually ask what you are doing. This is your opportunity to tell them your situation and ask for advice, information or contacts.

Unfortunately, too often those who are frantic to find a job, reconnect with former colleagues and friends, monopolize their time and annoy them. This behavior will destroy any networking opportunity you may have had.

Professional Organizations

Business organizations and associations offer many opportunities to network through their regular meetings, conferences and events. Members of these networks or organizations often know about upcoming jobs and other networking venues.

To maximize the benefits of business networking opportunities, you need to become an active member with organizations that interest you. Consider joining professional organizations or trade associations that fit your industry or job function.

There are functional networking groups for marketing, finance, human resources, engineering, etc. as well as industry based professional trade organizations such as the AEA (American Electronics Association), AMA (American Marketing Association) or ACG (Association for Corporate Growth), etc. Attending these functions will he assist you in building network connections with people that can help you find your next position.

Decide which group meetings you would like to attend, who you need to meet with and think about what you can offer others at the meetings. Get involved. When you join organizations, become a visible contributor and members will get to know who you are.

Organize meetings, become an officer or volunteer and this will give others a chance to see your organizational and leadership skills. Be sure to arrange networking activities and schedule time every week. Serve on committees and make genuine efforts to help others whenever possible. They will be willing to assist you in return. You'll become valuable to the organization and it will increase your visibility.

Locate Network Groups

To locate network groups in your local area, Google "network meetings" along with the name of your city and state. Network meeting locations, dates and times can also be found in your local newspaper or in business journals. There are plenty to choose from. Make sure to network with employed business people as well as those that are unemployed. Schedule regular dates to attend meetings and try to meet with different groups and associations.

If you are looking for a new opportunity or are unemployed, never ask for a job in a network setting. Set expectations that although you are job hunting, you are seeking advice and direction for your job search. Be sure to convey that you don't expect them to have a job for you or know about one. By setting expectations up front, the person is likely to be more at ease. This alleviates any uncomfortable expectations and allows the contact to relax, be more engaged and helpful.

Tradeshow Networking

One of the best places to network is at industry tradeshows, especially for sales, marketing, engineering and management people. Tradeshows provide an ideal venue for face to face meetings and quite often have senior managers in attendance with the potential to hire you. Find out what tradeshows will be in your area in advance of the schedule. A good source of listings for all types of tradeshows is provided on-line by the Trade Show News Network (tsnn.com).

What makes tradeshows a great place to network is that they are typically geared to specific industries. Tradeshows often post openings knowing that the room is full of potential hires with relevant industry experience. Be sure to do the research to locate shows that fit your current or target industry.

Some tradeshows will allow you to attend the exhibits for free by pre-registering while others charge a fee. To get around the entry fee, ask former colleagues if they can provide you with a guest badge for the exhibits. A guest badge can save you hundreds of dollars. If you want to save money, be sure to do the research on each show you are considering. Make sure you know what the cost to attend is before you show up.

While you are in the exhibit hall, stop by the booths and introduce yourself. Ask them if they know anyone in their company that might be looking for someone with your expertise or skill set. When they ask, 'what is your expertise or skill set", it's the perfect opportunity to deliver your *"elevator statement"*. Be sure to leave them with your business card, and follow-up immediately after the show.

Volunteering

One of the most effective forms of networking is volunteering. Get involved with a church, synagogue, food bank, homeless shelter, hospital, scouting, or any other type of volunteer group. Becoming a volunteer not only benefits the organization but also benefits you.

When you participate as a volunteer, you gain an opportunity to demonstrate your skills and abilities to others (organizing, project management, communication skills, finance, etc.). When others in the organization learn about you and your skills, you receive the benefit of building relationships with others who could potentially recommend you.

For some, volunteering takes them of their comfort zone and that is understandable. Step out of your comfort zone - join groups, participate on committees, and volunteer. Don't make the mistake of missing volunteer opportunities. I have heard a few candidates say; *"I don't have time to volunteer…I'm too busy looking for a job"*. Reality is, volunteering is networking to find a job!

Choosing Networking Groups

To be efficient, choose your network groups wisely. You are looking for people who could introduce you to someone in the companies you would like to work at or your target industries. Here are some things to consider:

- ❏ How often does the networking group meet?
- ❏ How much of your time will the group require?
- ❏ How committed do you feel to this type of group?

Pick at least three types of groups to consider:

1. A peer group for brainstorming, education and commiserating
2. A group of prospects that includes your ideal target market – people who interact with your target companies and target market.
3. A professional business group where you can boost your credentials through certification and your online presence via the memberships website.
4. A church or religious group that helps others, both functionally and spiritually.

Personal Networking Meetings

After meeting people at network events, set up follow-up meetings with people that could potentially help you. Before meeting with any person or group, consider what your objective is. In other words, meet with a purpose. You may be looking for contacts within companies or you may want to learn about other networking groups that may benefit you. You are there to build a relationship so be prepared to ask the right questions.

Set up meetings using LinkedIn or email for written correspondence and confirmation. If you are uncomfortable calling, create a script for your telephone conversations. Ask for advice, information about people that work at a target company or ask for a personal assessment on some subject matter. Make sure you have clarity on how someone can help you. Look to get introductions to key people within your target companies. Don't be afraid to ask for assistance and guidance.

Introductions and Recommendations

Introductions are a large part of networking. If someone you've met knows a person that could provide information about a position or company, you would certainly appreciate an introduction, right? Unfortunately, people often avoid making *introductions* because they think they are *recommending* someone. Let's make sure we understand the difference:

An *"introduction"* is connecting 2 individuals to each other for the purpose of networking. It is NOT a recommendation or a referral! An introduction is made when you do not know or barely know the 2 individuals. It's simply a method to make the connection. Good networkers understand this and are not afraid to make introductions and connections.

A *"recommendation"* is very different. When you know someone well enough and are comfortable with their skills, knowledge, character, etc., you might recommend them to someone. When you recommend someone, you should be able to provide details about why you are recommending them.

Follow-ups

Building relationships is not a one-time thing. After meeting with someone, send them a thank you note for their time. You may want to consider using email to send a personal update when appropriate. The important thing is to continue to nurture relationships by staying in communication.

Track Your Network Contacts

As we discussed in the chapter on Targeting Companies, develop a list of 25 companies that you would like to work for. Share the list with your contacts and ask them if they know anyone that works at any of the companies on your list. Follow-up by contacting the person referred. Ask your contacts for suggestions on other companies that you should also consider.

Tracking contact information is important to ensure you keep in touch with contacts on a regular basis. The simplest method to accomplish this is to keep collected business cards in some type of business card holder and put each person's contact information in your outlook or address book. Outlook's calendar can also help to schedule a follow-up with each person every 2 or 3 months to stay connected and continue to add value to that relationship.

Another method is to create a Microsoft excel or other spreadsheet template that tracks the name of the person, their contact number, e-mail, company name, date you last contacted them and comments. You should also use it to track the companies / jobs you applied for, what resume / materials were sent, next steps, etc.

CRM (Customer Relationship Management) programs are more

sophisticated than simple spreadsheets and provide greater detail and the ability to track scheduling with reminders. Even though CRM software is designed around a sales process for business, it can be applied to a job search because the product being sold is you! There are CRM programs and apps that can be adapted to monitor job search / networking progress and stay well organized.

If you are considering CRM for tracking network contacts and job searches, www.jibberjobber.com provides a unique and productive internet based tool to organize and manage this process. It tracks personal and professional relationships; target companies and jobs you apply to. JibberJobber.com is modeled after CRM (Customer Relationship Management) software to track the specifics details with contacts but unlike CRM, is designed specifically for a job search process. The company refers to this concept as a "Career Management" tool and jibberjobber.com is definitely worth consideration.

Ranking Your Contacts

I suggest you classify people you meet into one of 3 categories:

Category A – People who are interested in meeting with you and who seem genuinely interested in helping.

Category B - People who may be interested in meeting with you and who seem somewhat interested in helping.

Category C - People who aren't interested in you and only want to meet people who will do something for them.

Obviously, you'll want to work with the A & B types but it's good to note where people stand at in building relationships.

Monitor Your Progress

Be sure to track your activities in some type of chart or matrix. Set and track goals for each day and week. This will keep you on track in your networking efforts. Make sure you set realistic networking goals and measure them. Stick to your schedule and plan.

Progress Monitoring Chart

Activity	Goal	Daily	Weekly
Networking Events	Attend 2 events per week		2
New Contacts / Leads	Meet 10 new contacts	2	10
Networking Phone Calls	Follow-up calls	5	25
One-on-One Meetings	Network time with others	1	5
Target Company Research	Research companies	1	5
Informational Interviews	Approaching companies to network		2

Figure 11-2: Progress Monitoring Chart

Remember to strengthen your network connections by building trust. Become a resource for others and keep a positive attitude!

Step 3: Communicate Your Value — How To Work With Recruiters

Chapter 12

WORKING WITH RECRUITERS

Any highly skilled professional searching for a job should take advantage of the opportunity to work with professional recruiting firms. Recruiters have opportunities that are not publicly available and may only be listed through their search firm.

Recruiters can be a great resource for candidates who have skills or related industry experience that match a recruiters search criteria. For the right candidate, a recruiter can make an introduction and provide inside knowledge of a company's culture. When the employer decides to make you an offer for the position, the recruiter can also assist the parties with salary negotiation.

Before you work with a recruiter, it is important to understand the various types of recruiters and what searches they conduct. Here are some of the differences:

- **Retained Search** – Retained searches are typically used to locate candidates for high level executive positions such as a CEO, President, Vice President, etc. During a retained search, the recruiter receives an upfront payment from the employer and obtains exclusive rights to find the ideal candidate match for the position. "Pedigree" recruiting firms such as *Korn/Ferry*, *Spencer Stuart*, etc. specialize in these high-level searches. However, retained searches are also awarded to smaller firms that have an established reputation for delivering quality candidates. For example, *Impact Hiring Solutions* has been one of the most highly sought retained search recruiters in southern California.

- **Contingency Search** – Contingency searches typically range from mid-level or specialty skill positions up to management or executive positions. In a contingency search, payment is only made after the candidate is hired. For this reason, there may be multiple recruiters searching and presenting candidates to the same company for the same position. Contingency recruiters often surf the internet to find open positions and *"pitch"* employers with candidates from their inventory pool. Contingency searches move faster because there are multiple recruiters competing for the same open positions and the positions are typically lower level than retained search positions.

- **Agencies** - Temporary staffing agencies are also considered recruiters. These agencies fill an important role for employers, locating temporary workers to complete assignments or fill in for missing personnel. To be successful, agencies must be able to present qualified candidates quickly to an employer. Temp agency positions are generally lower level jobs such as executive assistants, customer service reps or project specialists. However, some firms specialize in higher level temporary staffing, filling management or executive level assignments. If a hiring company recognizes that a temp is a strong performer, a temporary position may become permanent.

- **Consulting Firms** – There are recruiters who specialize in finding candidates for temporary consulting assignments. They focus on finding talent with specific industry, functional or technical expertise. Consulting positions are usually temporary and these search firms look for qualified consultants who prefer this over permanent employment.

Beware of Scammers

Keep in mind that almost all searches are paid for by the employer. While there are many legitimate career management and career coaching firms, there are some that are only interested in taking your money and will provide you little or nothing in return.

Avoid "*career management firms*" who offer career advice and a "guarantee" to find you a job for **a fee**. Be aware that these pseudo "recruiters" will most likely never deliver on the "guarantee" to find you a job after you've paid them.

Working with recruiters

If you decide to work with recruiters, you must first recognize that recruiters are good people trying to do a job. It is important to remember, they work for the hiring employer, not you! They only get paid when they fill the position. Therefore, the first rule in working with recruiters is to understand that recruiters find people for jobs, not jobs for people!

Recruiters are in business to make money and will only be interested in working with you if you have the skills and experience that match one of their searches. If they can't place you, they can't make money. If you don't have a background that matches the skills they need for a search, the recruiter has little incentive to work with you. They would damage their own reputation if they attempted to convince a hiring manager that you are the best candidate when you are not. Don't take it personally!

Since candidates are the "product" they offer to employers, recruiters often build an "inventory" of potential candidates. If you are a good candidate, recruiters may want to keep you in their database should a search open up that closely matches your skill set.

If the recruiter recognizes that you have a unique skill set or are a candidate with a strong track record, a recruiter may offer to "represent" you. By doing so, they may shop your resume around to several companies.

Finding recruiters

Start by looking for recruiters that specialize in placements for your specific industry; i.e. medical device, aerospace, defense, etc. You might also search for recruiters that specialize in specific functional areas; finance, marketing, engineering, IT, etc.

Search for recruiters' profiles online – Thousands of recruiters have profiles on networking sites.

LinkedIn.com is a great source for finding recruiter firms. They carry over 90,000 recruiter profiles and most of them list a specialty. It's free to join LinkedIn although the advanced features require paid membership. To find recruiters' profiles, search LinkedIn for "recruitment" and "agencies".

Customdatabanks.com is an aggregate online site that lists information about search firms, venture capitalists, etc. The site offers a subscription database with access to this type of information.

BlueSteps.com offers continual exposure to a database of thousands of recruiters from retained search firms who are members of the AESC (Association of Executive Search and Leadership Consultants). Their core membership fee is a lifetime benefit and costs $289.00. Additional premium services are included for the first six months of membership, then renew on an annual basis.

Search recruiter directories online - Here are some online directories: recruiterlink.com, onlinerecruitersdirectory.com, searchfirm.com and i-recruit.com.

Library resource recruiter directories - Your local library has other resources available at no charge. Most major cities have some type of business journal newspaper which is geared specifically to news about local businesses. Business journals profile companies, show mergers and acquisitions, list charitable events, and a host of other topics.

For example, in the Southern California market, there are three different papers; the San Diego Business Journal, the Orange County Business Journal and the LA Business Journal. These publications typically provide an annual "book of lists" which contains a ranking list of local companies as well as recruiting firms by size and revenue. While you can always pay for your own local business journal subscription, they typically can be viewed at your local library for free.

Networking is another source to locate recruiters. Solicit information by asking peers which recruiters they have worked with. Ask for the names of recruiters they would personally recommend. At network meetings, ask hiring managers which recruiters they use to fill similar positions. After receiving a name, do research the recruiter on-line to learn more about them.

Make yourself visible to recruiters on-line

To locate qualified candidates quickly and efficiently, the recruiters tool of choice is LinkedIn. In fact, the surveys show that over 90% of recruiters now search for candidates online or using LinkedIn. Most recruiters pay for a LinkedIn premium subscription which gives them far greater access to details about qualified candidates. Keep in mind that human resource departments are also using LinkedIn to data mine for the best qualified matches.

To increase your chances of being found through internet searches, you'll need to make sure that recruiters and hiring managers can easily find you online. Make sure your LinkedIn profile is complete and up to date.

Recruiters search LinkedIn for keywords, titles, industries and locations. When your profile is complete and contains these keywords and specific information, you'll have a much better chance of being found.

Contacting Recruiters

E-mail works well and is easier to use but paper resumes may have a slightly better chance of being looked at, simply because they receive so many emails. If you send a paper resume, make sure to also include a cover letter explaining what you are looking for and include your contact information.

If one of your network contacts knows a recruiter and is willing to make an introduction, even better. You will have a much better chance of getting a call back from the recruiter out of courtesy to that individual. Recruiters call back when they know or trust the person providing the referral.

This does not apply to an "acquaintance" but some someone who actually has a relationship with the recruiter. We're talking about a former client or a previous placement. Utilize your network contacts and LinkedIn to locate a someone who has a relationship with the recruiter who might be able to help.

Recruiters, like employers, check criteria "boxes" to screen people quickly. This means that they are looking for specific things and if you don't have them, the boxes remain unchecked and you're out of contention. Here are some of the "boxes" recruiters will most likely look to check:

- *Level of Position* – If the recruiter is searching for someone at a director level and you have never been a director, you're out of consideration.

- *Industry* – If the recruiter specializes in placing candidates in the medical device industry and your background is in aerospace, you're probably out of consideration.

- *Job Function* – If the recruiter is searching for someone with a strong marketing background and your background is mostly in sales, you're probably out of consideration.

- *Location* – If you don't already live in the area, it most likely you will be out of consideration, unless the position includes a relocation package.

- *Job Turnover* – If your resume shows a lot of turnover in the last 4 or 5 years, most recruiters view you as having a low probability succeeding long term which may take you out of the running. Recruiters have something called a "fall-off ratio" which refers to the ratio of candidates they placed that didn't work out and are let go.

  Most recruiters provide some type of guarantee that if the candidate does not work out within a certain time period, they will offer a refund or agree to find another candidate. The last thing the recruiter wants to do is have a candidate "fall off". Therefore, they will avoid anyone that they perceive to have a track record of turnover.

Speaking with a Recruiter

As with any potential job opportunity, it is best to call the recruiter to personally follow-up on your initial mailer. Making personal contact is always helpful in selling yourself. Don't give up if the recruiter doesn't get back to you. They are not trying to be rude; it's usually a time constraint. Be persistent but not annoying and sooner or later you will catch them in the office.

When you get the recruiter on the phone via a cold call, begin by showing them courtesy and ask them if it's a good time to talk. If it is not, request an alternate time to call back as their time is valuable and should be respected. Also, ask them what their preferred communication method is. Whatever you do, don't immediately go into a long-winded speech about how great you are as you will turn them off. Recruiters are pros at spotting talent and recognizing those that exaggerate or outright lie.

When the Recruiter is Interested in You

If a recruiter is interested in you as a potential match for a position, it is important to listen and analyze everything they say. The recruiter knows what the company is looking for and is consistently evaluating you to see if you are a cultural fit as well as ensuring you have the job skills to meet the client's requirements.

At the same time, you can evaluate the recruiter by querying them on the phone. By asking questions, you'll be able to tell if the recruiter is interested in you. If they are willing to spend time with you and share information, you'll know they are interested.

The recruiter can also provide you with insight on what it would be like to work for the company. They can also provide the steps and timeframe involved in the hiring process. Many candidates simply answer the questions asked by the recruiter and don't take advantage of the opportunity to partner with them through interactive dialog. This may also help differentiate you from other candidates if the recruiter likes you.

Be sure to ask the recruiter if they will provide you with feedback about your candidacy as the process moves along. Learning information on what others have to say about you, good or bad, will help you be a better candidate.

Recruiters don't typically share negative feedback because the candidate will attempt to convince the recruiter why the feedback is not warranted. Let them know that the any and all feedback will help you improve.

Set your own expectations and learn how to work within recruiters. In any case, get to know the local search firms and start building a relationship. Take advantage of the benefits of working with professional recruiters to *shorten your job search*.

Step 4 — Win The Interview

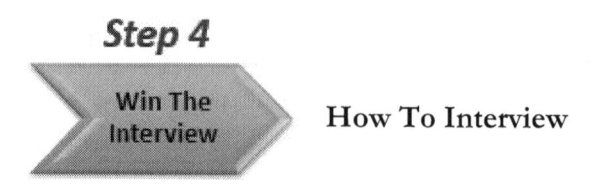

How To Interview

Chapter 13

WINNING THE JOB INTERVIEW

When you finally get to that interview congratulations, you have succeeded with your marketing. You've invested a significant amount of time and resources, all for the purpose of landing an interview. Something in your resume, LinkedIn profile, networking connection, etc. has caught the eye of a hiring manager and has convinced them that you are a potentially good fit for the position and warrant serious consideration.

However, just because you are moving on to the interview, does not mean you will get the job. If you want to succeed you will need to prepare and make an impression. Keep this in mind:

It's not the smartest or the best qualified candidate that gets the position. It's the one who interviews the best!

Anatomy of an Interview

There are 3 parts to a job interview; the *opening*, the *middle* and the *close*. Each part is important but the 2 most influential parts of the interview are the *opening* and the *close*. **Believe it or not, most interviews are decided within the first 5 minutes; simply because you made or did not make an impression!**

The close is also important because it provides an opportunity for redemption if something was not perceived well during the interview. The following graphic looks at these 3 interview stages:

Stages of an Interview

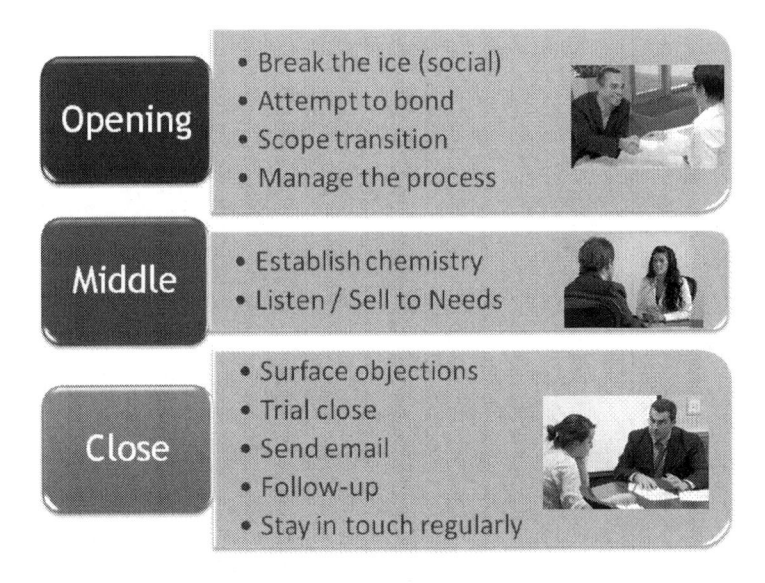

Opening
- Break the ice (social)
- Attempt to bond
- Scope transition
- Manage the process

Middle
- Establish chemistry
- Listen / Sell to Needs

Close
- Surface objections
- Trial close
- Send email
- Follow-up
- Stay in touch regularly

Figure 12-1: Stages of an Interview

What Employers Are Really Looking for in an Interview

An interview is an exploratory process between you and the interviewer.

What interviewer's typically look for are two things; do you "fit" into their company culture, and second, whether or not you should be eliminated as a candidate!

Interviewers are digging for are what I call *"hidden attributes"* or *qualities* that you show during the interview process. Here are some examples of what they may be looking for. These are never spoken, they are perceived.

Decision-making style: Did you use facts or hunches, emotions in your responses?

Responses: Clarity of thought, appropriate language, did you interrupt, did you listen and respond to the questions as they were asked.

Writing Skill: Correspondence, misspellings, grammar, typos.

Interpersonal Skills: Attitude, tact, poise, sociability, perceived ability to work with groups.

Background: Relating to peers, reporting to superiors and handling subordinates (if you are in supervisory positions)

Interests: Community involvement, volunteering, hobbies.

Leadership: If you are in a supervisory position - ability to influence others. These are validated through situational questions like:

- Have you ever fired someone and why?
- What makes a good manager?

Achievement Record: Identify 3 significant achievements and probe. Exaggeration? Energy, vitality, perseverance.

Promotions: Why did you receive your last promotion?

Sense of Direction: Goal setting, understanding the cultural environment, company industry.

- ☐ Why did you take your last job?

- ☐ How did you choose this company?

Remember, the interview is really about establishing a "cultural connection". During the interview, you may be asked questions to test your knowledge to ensure the interviewer that you are qualified the way they perceived you are.

How to Prepare - Before the Interview

I cannot understate that ***preparing for the interview is just as important as the actual interview!*** There is a great deal of preparation to do before long before the interview begins.

Think of interviewing as competing in the Olympics. Athletes prepare by training for years with incredible dedication and focus on one thing – winning at one event. They know that to win gold, they need to outperform other equally gifted athletes right down to the end. After all the preparation and training, the difference between winning the gold or silver may come down to a fraction of a second.

Think of your interview in the same way. You'll need extensive preparation and dedication focusing on one thing - winning the job. The following preparation can make you a champion at interviewing!

Research the company

Most hiring managers can usually tell within the first five minutes whether or not you are the right fit for the job. One of these early qualifiers may come when the employer tests what you know about their company. If you don't do the research, how can you possibly have an intelligent conversation about the company, its goals, or its culture? They don't expect you to have inside knowledge, but demonstrating that you've done your homework will go a long way in impressing the interviewer.

Start with researching the company & the industry. Focus on understanding their problems. Learn about their products and services and understand how the company is doing financially. Much of this information can be found on the web or on the company's own website, typically under "about us". LinkedIn also provides generic information about companies. More information on companies can also be found by using public library sources such as:

- Reference USA (referenceusa.com/)
- Hoovers (Dun & Bradstreet - hoovers.com/)
- These sites can even provide information on privately held companies

Understand the Culture

Look for information about the company culture by tapping into your LinkedIn network to find someone who is currently working there or has previously worked there. If you don't have a first level LinkedIn connection, get one of your first level contacts to make an introduction to someone who is a second or third level connection. Ask them about the company's culture and learn about the company's management style. Here are some things to ask about the culture:

- Is the company culture <u>team oriented</u> or is it <u>driven from the top leader down</u>?

- How long has the person you contacted worked there? If everyone you connect with has only been there a short time, there may be a culture of turnover.

- How do they like working there? If they left the company, why did they leave?

Find out if your network contact(s) know the hiring manager. Look for an insider's perspective and background information on the people you'll be interviewing with. What do you have in common with the interviewer(s)?

In addition to speaking with insiders, research the people you will be interviewing with using LinkedIn or with a Google or Bing search. You may also want to look on information sites like mylife.com, zabasearch.com, etc. to learn more about their background.

Don't ever forget that an interview is competitive and there is only going to be one winner in the end. Find out what problems the company is facing and give them reason to think that you are the person that can solve them. Instead of just hoping to succeed in the interview, create a strategy for the interview in advance.

Are You Emotionally Ready?

It's very important to be emotionally ready for an interview! When you are not working, every dollar counts and you are eager to get hired to fill the financial and emotional void. Depending on your personality, some handle the stress of transition better than others.

Look in the mirror. If you are someone who is having difficulties adjusting to being in transition, you need to get it together emotionally before you even consider going to an interview. I have seen and interviewed candidates who begged for jobs during the interview, eliminating themselves instantly from consideration.

When you are smiling and feel well suited for a job opportunity, by all means go for it. If you feel overwhelmed, stressed or confused, consider setting this opportunity aside and look for another position that would be a better match for your capabilities and experience at a later time.

Only when you're equipped with a practical sense of direction and emotional clarity can you walk into an interview and establish a good rapport with a hiring manager.

Prepare To Discuss Your Qualifications

To demonstrate your value, you must be ready to respond to a variety of questions in real time.

To prepare, start by looking back throughout your entire career and <u>list every accomplishment you have ever achieved</u> no matter how insignificant. You'll need to be able to recite them verbatim when asked a relevant question.

To communicate these accomplishments, we'll rely on the PAR statements we previously discussed. These PAR statements should be explained as *"power stories"*.

As you recall from Chapter 5 on *"Developing Your Personal Brand", power stories* are challenges you faced and overcame. During the interview you must be able to clearly and concisely articulate your accomplishments using the P.A.R. method stating the Problem, the Action, and the Results. "Power stories" should be 60 seconds to 2 or 3 minutes at most.

RECAP:
The P.A.R. Methodology to Communicate
"Power Stories"

Describe the **PROBLEM** you faced	Describe the **ACTION** you took to solve the problem	What **RESULTS** were achieved from your course of action
What problem or situation did you deal with? *Relational, organizational, functional...*	What skills did you use to solve the problem? *Analyzed, reviewed, created, collaborated...*	What difference did you make? *Reduced cost, increased revenue, improved efficiency, satisfied customer...*

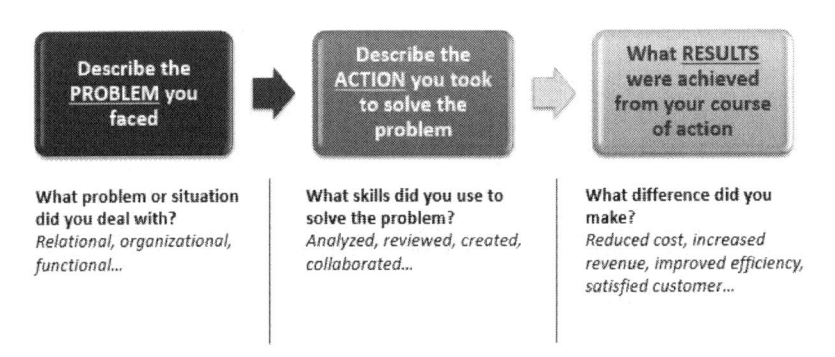

Figure 12-2: PAR Methodology

1. Start with statements that describe a **PROBLEM** or situation you faced and dealt with (relational, organizational, functional, etc.). Focus on the 2-3 top things that you want the interviewer to remember about you.

2. Follow this with a description of the **ACTION** you took to address the problem. What skills did you use? What type of action did you take (analyzed, reviewed, created, collaborated, etc.)? How did you respond to others involved (influenced, lead , managed, supported,, etc.? Be specific but not overly detailed. What processes did you develop, improve, implement or control? Were these administrative, operational, etc.?

3. The most important part of the power story is the **RESULT(S)** you accomplished. What difference did you make through your action (reduced cost, increased revenue, improved efficiency, saved time, satisfied the customer, etc.)

For this **results** portion, be sure to *quantify* as much as possible as "measurable" results; (Cost reduction, time saving, productivity increase, improved morale, etc.).

Practice your "power stories" using 3 x 5 cards with questions.

Power Story Examples

As you applied for a *Director of Marketing position,* the hiring manager asks:

"Tell me about a situation where you reorganized your department that had a positive impact on the business".

This is a very specific question where the interviewer is looking to understand your capabilities as a manager. More importantly, they need to learn if you are a leader that is not afraid to make changes.

Your *power story* response;

PROBLEM statement: "When I was hired as Director of Marketing at Bogus Corporation, the company hadn't launched a new product in over 2 years. It was clear that the company needed to develop new products to stay competitive in the market."

ACTION statement: "The first action I took was to meet with the members of the product marketing team to better understand what each of their roles and responsibilities were and what percentage of their time was actually spent on product development.

After interviewing the team, I learned that the product managers were spending most of their time responding to calls and following up on problems requested by the sales team.

Based on this information, I reorganized the department into upstream and downstream marketing, where the upstream people focused solely on product development and the downstream people worked with the field sales team to respond to their needs.

RESULT statement: "This organizational change resulted in launching 2 new products in the same year, improved overall team morale and produced an 11% increase in revenue year over year".

Map Your Power Stories to the Job Description

Now that you are ready to deliver responses about your lifetime of accomplishments, focus on finding which ones which relate to the specific responsibilities of the position.

Closely review the job description. Using the job description as a reference, map each skill and experience request to something you have done that is similar or relevant. Write down how your accomplishments mapped to the requirements.

Based on your company research, think about how would you address their problems? (Make some assumptions based on their priority issues). Practice how you would address each in a *"power story" (Power stories* must be relevant to the employer and company).

From this process, develop 2-3 questions that you can ask the interviewer.

Since most people do not have the EXACT experience the position is asking for, be prepared to use relevant experience to demonstrate that you have the skill sets needed. Here is a simple example.

Requirement: 4 Years Sales Experience Required – "While I don't have experience selling this particular product, I have relevant sales experience as a waiter for 5 years, where I up-sell customers on food service products to increase my tips /commission"

Preparation Before the Interview

Now that you have compiled your prior accomplishments, mapped them to the job description and understand how to communicate them, get ready for the actual interview.

As we did before, begin with preparation! If possible, drive by the interview location the day before so you know exactly where it is and how long it takes to get there from your home or hotel, etc. Double check to make sure you know the time, the place, and the interviewer's name and title.

Plan your appearance by determining what you are going to wear in advance. More and more companies today have casual attire. However, even companies with a casual dress code will likely expect you to show up with a suit and tie. Unless the company specifies otherwise when in doubt, dress for success!

For women, use good sense and dress with the appropriate business attire. I have seen women who showed up looking like they were going to a night club. They did not make a favorable impression. Employers are looking for the person who is the best fit for the job. Look, act and be professional!

Prepare your documentation

Bring copies of your resume with you and <u>don't assume they already have a copy</u>. Bring along interview notes, a post interview packet and any other documents you feel are appropriate. Some candidates have brought prewritten follow-up letters ready to drop off in the company mail immediately after the interview.

Be on Time

Leave early and plan to arrive 15 to 30-minutes early. If you arrive early enough, go across the street, get a cup of coffee and wait. Take that time to review the job description, your power stories and other materials for the interview.

Be sure to account for heavy traffic, accidents, flat tires or other things that can go wrong. Showing up late for an interview may be the quickest way of getting eliminated as a candidate, no matter what the excuse. It sends a message to the employer that you don't plan well or that you may end up being habitually late.

After Arriving

After you arrive, go to the restroom and turn off your cell phone. Looking down at your phone or reading text messages in an interview will not go over well so turn it off! 15 minutes before the interview, let them know you've arrived.

Connect with people quickly – smile, engage the receptionist (if they are not too busy – if they are don't annoy them) - *make a positive impression.* When you arrive in the lobby don't sit - *stand* to project your presence. Give an appearance of energy and stay alert.

Turn on your visual receptors - Look at awards on the wall, make observations of the environment. These things may come in handy during the interview. For example, noting awards in the lobby might allow you to complement the company's achievements during a discussion. (For a marketing position) *"I see that bogus agency has won 5 CLEO awards, that's impressive"*.

The Interview Opening

Chances are you will be escorted to the manager's office or the area in which the interview will take place. Be friendly and courteous to everyone, including the receptionist or the person that escorts you in. Making a positive impression with EVERYONE is very important. The hiring manager may take stock in whatever the receptionist says about you. You never know!

The First 5 Minutes

The first five minutes are critical. As humans, we are all "wired differently" and react quickly to different types of stimuli. Sometimes it's just a feeling, but it stays with you throughout the meeting and eventually, decides the fate of the candidate.

There are things you can do to make a good first impression. Walk in the door and look confident. Be friendly, but not over the top. Look professional and polished. Be responsive, not silent.

Greet the interviewer(s) with a firm handshake and a smile. A confident and friendly smile says you are comfortable. Look them in the eye and introduce yourself (Don't look down or look distracted – this shows lack of self-confidence). Listen carefully to the employers' introductions and especially to their names, titles etc. Show them you are energetic and interested.

Wait for them to sit and then you do. Be sure you say, "thank you for the opportunity". Maintain good posture and keep eye contact. This signals the employer that you are interested in the opportunity right from the start.

Lead the conversation by being personable. Engage in an early discussion by asking questions with something like; *"So how long have you been with the company"*. Have a conversation with the interviewer and make it interactive. However, don't get too personal or get comfortable. They are listening to every word you say.

This "ice breaking" is an important part of the beginning of the interview as it makes you more likeable and establishes a human connection. Most employers don't like "robots" who simply follow orders. Managers prefer people who think for themselves so make an early impression.

Interview Guidelines

Make the interview a two-way discussion but don't take over the interview. Too many candidates are nervous and want to tell the interviewer everything there is to know about them. This is a classic mistake and can cost you the job.

Be interactive during the discussion and let the interviewer lead. Assess how the person is communicating with you and watch how they respond. Are they engaged, looking at you or scuffling papers? Adjust your interaction as needed to get them to reengage.

Listen and Learn

You would be surprised just how many managers and supervisors have never been trained to interview candidates. Take advantage of this by obtaining key information which can help you. For example, as the interview progresses, ask the interviewer to "describe the ideal candidate". This will help you strategize your responses in real time.

Be a good listener and *most of all listen carefully to each question!!* Answer each question that is asked. **According to recruiters, this is one of the most common mistakes candidates make during an interview**! Don't answer with something general that you want to say. Make it situational and address the interviewers' questions. Try to maximize each opportunity by demonstrating your achievements with short and medium length *power story* responses.

Do not interrupt when an employer is talking!! Although candidates are nervous and want to make an impression, interrupting the interviewing when they are speaking sends a message that you don't respect the manager's authority or that you are not confident.

Here are a few interview "don'ts".

- *Don't exaggerate or lie. Your life is online and readily available. Background and reference checks make it easier than ever to catch you.*

- *Don't make negative comments about anything or criticize past employers.*

- *Don't project aggression or hostility*

- *Don't appear emotional or subjective*

- *Don't over talk when you answer questions or fill in dead air with rambling!*

- *Don't discuss salary, vacation, time off, commute or related items.*

- *Don't respond before the person finishes asking the question!*

Be prepared to answer the "cliché" questions

As I mentioned earlier, most managers are not highly skilled interviewers. There are management courses available on how to probe candidates to learn hidden details. However, most managers simply don't know how to probe. Instead, they ask the "cliché" questions. These are common questions that have been used time and time again.

Here are some examples of typical cliché questions:

- Tell me about yourself
- What are your greatest strengths?
- What are your biggest weaknesses?
- What can you offer that someone else cannot?
- What are your 3 most important career accomplishments?
- How would you describe yourself?
- Why should we hire you?
- Describe the biggest crisis in your life
- What is unique about you?
- What do you think determines a person's progress with a good company?
- Who has exercised the greatest influence on you?
- What have you done to increase your personal development?
- What was the most useful criticism ever received?

- What is the biggest change you have made in the past ten years?
- Can you work well under stress?
- Are you a team player?
- What are the things that motivate you?
- What have you done that shows initiative?
- Are you willing to take calculated risks?
- Can you establish effective methods and procedures?
- Give me an example of how you are resourceful?
- What has been your biggest challenge?
- Describe a team project where you are proud of the team results as well as your personal contribution.
- Describe a difficult situation and the progress you made to turn it around
- Give me 3 qualities that are helping you get ahead and 3 qualities needing work to achieve my goals.
- What is the largest number of people you have ever managed?

Rest assured, you will most likely be asked some of these questions during an interview so you need to prepare for all of them. It is important to prepare yourself but don't memorize a word for word answer.

If you try to memorize a response to a question like "what is your greatest strength", you will simply blurt out a canned response. At the same time the interviewer will find it unusual that you answered the question so quickly with little or no time to think about a response.

Instead, pause for a moment before you answer like you are thinking through your response. Relate the answer to the job you are applying for. For example, if the position is a Customer Service Representative, your greatest strength should somehow relate to customer service. You could be the greatest copy writer on the planet, but if the skill is not relevant to the position, it is not worth boasting about it.

Types of Interviews

While most people are familiar with the traditional face to face hiring manager interview, you may find yourself facing different types of interviews that you are not familiar with. These include telephone interviews, video interviews, group or panel interviews and situational or behavioral interviews.

Telephone Interviews

Telephone interviews provide a means for a company to pre-qualify you over the phone before bringing you in for a face to face discussion. It is very common to have human resources conduct the first line of telephone screening interviews. Since human resources doesn't know the explicit details of every job in every department, they generalize based on what is written in the job description. This means they simply "check boxes" to pre-qualify your expertise and gauge your interest.

Phone interviews are also used when a company is considering multiple candidates. This is especially true in situations where relocation is offered. The phone interview tells the employer whether to spend the time and money to bring you in for an in-person interview.

It is important to note that a phone interview is just as critical as a first round, in-person interview. Taking a phone interview for granted can easily get you eliminated from contention. Your goal should be to make a strong impression and to get past this stage without being eliminated.

Telephone interviews are difficult because there are no visual cues to measure how you are doing. There's no eye contact to make and no facial expression or no body language to read. The only "feel" you get is from the other person's voice and intonation. By contrast, the interviewer's impression of you is also gauged by your voice and intonation.

Preparation, which is always essential prior to any interview, is the one thing that can help you get past this stage when you can't see what the interviewer is doing. Before the interview call, find a quiet, private place to have your telephone discussion, one that has a table or desk surface in front of you.

One advantage you have is that you can layout lots of notes and cheat sheets to read from and the interviewer won't know this (unless you make a lot of noise rustling through your papers)! Spread your interview notes and cheat sheets out so you can glance down to make key points.

Be sure to have a copy of your resume and the job description nearby. Don't use your computer to look at notes or you may find yourself searching through pages of documents while you are trying to converse! Print them out so you can find them quickly in advance.

Be sure to have a pen and paper so that you can take notes. Your typed notes should include your list of accomplishments, PAR statements and how all your skills relate to the job (this assumes you have done the research on the company before the call.

During the call, standup, walk around and smile. Project a positive attitude and presence. As you would in any interview, listen carefully and answer the specific question that was asked. All these things make a big difference in how you will be perceived.

Video Interviews

Like telephone interviews, video interviews provide an economical method to pre-qualify you and decide whether to spend the time and money to bring you in to meet with the hiring manager or management team. Unlike telephone interviews, video allows the interviewer to watch your facial expressions and body language.

Video interviews may be conducted using the camera on your home computer with skype, facetime or something similar. The company may request that you go to their local, satellite office or to a firm that specializes in this type of video interviewing technology.

Just as the phone interview is, the video interview should be considered equal to a first round, in-person interview at the company's headquarters. Here again, your goal should be to make a strong impression and avoid being eliminated. Be conscious that you are projecting more of a smiling face than an intense or negative one.

Since the camera only shows a small visual, you do have the opportunity to layout your notes and cheat sheets to read from. Spread your interview notes and cheat sheets out so you can glance down to communicate your key points. Make sure you have a copy of your resume nearby.

Group / Panel Interviews

Hiring the wrong person can cost a company valuable time and resources.

To reduce the chances of a bad hire, group and panel interviews are becoming more common. The group / panel interview allows multiple people of varying levels and functions to listen to a candidate's responses to questions simultaneously. This format then allows the group to compare notes at a later time to see if there is a consensus on whether or not they liked the candidate.

What makes the group / panel interview challenging is the *group dynamic*. There are typically one or two individuals within the group that have the authority to make a decision on a candidate. Most of the rest simply go to the interview because they were asked to.

Because of this group dynamic, the actual interview can have many different interactive scenarios. For example, the "alpha" leaders may do all the talking or they may sit back and listen to what the group is asking. They may not pay attention or may drive the entire process. All of this makes it more difficult for the candidate to impress everyone on the panel.

It is important to note that whenever possible, find out all the names of the people you will be meeting with in advance. If you can obtain this information, (usually from HR or a manager you've been speaking with), take the time to research each person on LinkedIn or from other sources. From this research, you will have a better understanding of who the key individuals are before the group interview, especially to identify the "alpha" leaders.

Managing a Group / Panel Interview

Just as you would for a one on one interview, your initial approach is important in the way you walk in the door and carry yourself. Look confident, be friendly and act professional.

Greet the each of the interviewers on the panel with a firm handshake and a smile. Look each one of them in the eye and introduce yourself focusing on them. (Don't look at everyone else while you are shaking hands – this shows you don't respect them).

Listen carefully to the introductions and especially to each one of their names, titles etc. The best way to obtain this is ask them for business cards. If they don't have one, write their name and title down. This information is critical to be able to send follow-up notes.

Wait for all of them to sit and then you do. Be sure you say "thank you for the opportunity". Maintain good posture and keep eye contact will tell the employer you are interested in the company right from the start.

During the group interview – make eye contact with each person on the panel. Focus on the person asking the question but answer to the group. Even if the group seems cold, be warm to them. You should conduct yourself in the same manner as you would for any other interview.

Behavioral and Situational Interviews

Behavioral and situational interviews are similar as both are designed to help the interviewer better understand how a candidate will react under challenging circumstances. Interviewers may use behavioral questions to assess your past and future performance.

During behavioral interviews, candidates may be asked about things like their ability to work with others in difficult situations or with those who have clashing personalities. They may ask about past mistakes or how you wish you'd handled a situation differently with a colleague or client. How would your behavior change?

As you would for any interview and to prepare for behavioral interview questions, review the job posting in detail in advance and identify the position's key skill requirements.

For each skill requirement, identify a situation where you exhibited the required skill during your prior work or volunteer experience or extracurricular activity.

You should have "power stories" prepared and ready memorized using the PAR method for every core competency listed on the job posting. Preparing for this through in advance will help to enable your best responses during the interview.

Situational Interviews

While behavioral interview questions are focused on assessing your behavior based on your past experience, situational interview questions are designed to evaluate your ability to respond to hypothetical challenges. Situational questions provide the interviewer an opportunity to assess your problem-solving ability, values, and knowledge.

An interviewer may present you with a hypothetical situation related to a workplace issue and ask how you would respond. The interviewer will be evaluating your ability to address challenges and solve problems under pressure. Listen carefully to the questions and apply power stories using the PAR method as described earlier. You should demonstrate how to resolve the issue presented while highlighting your strengths.

The interviewer may also create an ethical dilemma and ask you how would address the situation. By posing ethical situations, the interviewer can evaluate your personal values and integrity based on your responses. Here again, stick with the high road in your responses and make sure you answer with the utmost integrity. If this is the type of company that is loose on honesty and integrity values (and there are some believe it or not), you may not want to work there anyway.

Interviewers use these types of questions to determine whether or not you will be a good fit for the position. Your past behavior and situational performance serves as a strong indicator of future performance. By asking you details about your prior professional experiences, interviewers can assess whether you possess the necessary skills for the position.

Closing the Interview

The "Closing" is a very important part of the interview. Near the end of the interview, employers will often ask; "Do you have any questions for me"? Asking closing questions is important and will show that you are a logical thinker who pays attention to detail.

To prepare for the interview close, make a list of questions and save them for the end.

Here are some examples of closing questions:

"What do you see as the immediate priorities in this position"?

"What are the long-term objectives for this position"?

"Can you tell me what the company's most important values are"?

"Why is this position open"? (Is this a new position or did someone leave?)

"What is the work environment like? Is it more collaborative or autonomous"?

"What's the most important aspect you're looking for in the person you hire"?

"What are the next steps"?

"When do expect to make a decision for this position"?

The Final Close

No matter what you are selling, (in this case the product is you), you must "close" the sale. As part of the close, you'll need to know if there are any final objections. To draw out any final objections from the interviewer, come right out and ask them for their opinion of you. Ask a question like:

"Have I demonstrated that I have all the skills and experience required for the position and can you let me know what you think of me as a candidate"?

Or - *"Based on what you've learned about me today, would you consider me for the position"?*

After asking the question, listen for the "BUT" – This provides a last chance opportunity to rebut a key issue that might not get you the job.

"I think you are a good candidate, BUT…."

After they have indicated what the "BUT" is, you have a moment to make them feel at ease about the objection.

Without asking, candidates often leave an interview thinking they have done well only to learn later they did not get the position. What's worse is they don't know why. Knowing any objection is a very important part of the interview close.

Here is an example of overcoming an objection:

Candidate: *"Have I demonstrated that I have all the skills and experience required for the position and can you let me know what you think of me as a candidate?"*

Interviewer: *"I think you are a very good candidate BUT, we were looking for someone who has an MBA in marketing for the product development manager position."*

Candidate: *"I understand and respect that. However, I would like to point out that I have over 5 years' experience in marketing including successfully developing products for the same medical device market segments. I believe my prior industry experience can bring value to your organization and I am willing to pursue an MBA".*

Candidate: *"Is that acceptable to you?"*

Listen to the response and watch the body language. This will give you a good indication of whether or not you've overcome the objection.

After the Interview

Immediately after the interview (even in your car in the parking lot), make notes of all the people you met with and what was discussed. This will help you refer back to the discussions to personalize your *thank you* responses.

Prepare your thank you note / letter as soon as possible. Your thank you can be a mailed letter, an e-mail or a hand-written card (same day within 24 hours). Feel free to mention key points or highlights in your note.

As a rule, do not send the same follow-up letter to multiple people. Often interviewers discuss candidates and receiving the same letter gives the perception that you did want to take the time to address each person individually. It sends a message that you are lazy or didn't care enough to send each interviewer a personal response.

A long delay in sending follow-up letters shows a lack of interest or that you work at a slow pace.

A word of caution about email follow-up notes. Keep in mind that the employer's e-mail system may flag your thank you email as just another piece of spam, especially when it comes from a yahoo, Gmail or other common domain address. **If the email never reaches them, they may perceive you as non-responsive, lazy or lacking in etiquette.**

Last of all, follow-up. Continue regular communication until they let you know that you are getting the position or they have filled it with someone else!

Step 5: Negotiate Your Salary

How To Negotiate Salary

Chapter 14

SALARY NEGOCIATION

It never ceases to amaze me why most candidates spend <u>the least amount of time</u> thinking or planning about the most important part of a job; their salary! When the job offer finally comes, negotiating salary is the most important thing you'll need to do. How much you make determines your lifestyle!

Think about how much money you need to live on <u>before</u> you apply for a position. Don't make the mistake of going through the entire interview process only to find you cannot afford to live on the salary offered.

In an earlier chapter, we discussed the importance of knowing what your fixed and discretionary expenses are. Your salary should be able to adequately cover these expenses. If it does not, it is due to one of two reasons; the position does not pay enough salary for you to live on or you are living beyond your financial means. In any case, learning how to negotiate your salary should be a high priority.

Too often during interviews, job applicants are unprepared when asked questions about salary. Not knowing how to answer the question; *"How much do you make"* can cost you the job, or if you do get hired, may result in you leaving thousands of dollars of salary on the table.

A Word of Caution

There is no universal knowledge that I can share that will determine how much an employer is actually willing to negotiate for salary and benefits! Every job and every company is different. What you can benefit from is an improved understanding of guidelines to consider in any salary negotiation.

As a rule, *the higher the level of position*, the greater the opportunity to negotiate for benefits. In addition to salary, I have provided a variety of benefits that may or may not be negotiable. The only one who can accurately assess your salary situation is you. Keep these suggestions in perspective as guidelines. Salary and benefits may or may not be negotiable in your particular situation.

Learn about the salary in advance

Most professional positions are salaried as opposed to hourly. This discussion applies to salaried positions.

To be able to know whether a job pays enough and to effectively negotiate salary, you need to know what the salary range of the position is BEFORE reaching the interview stage. Generally speaking, while companies have a number for your position's salary in the budget, they usually don't have an exact dollar amount set in stone at the time of negotiation.

Employers typically have a salary range associated with each job classification and description. For example; salary band "S4" ranges from $62,000 to $78,000 and is usually determined by job performance and / or years of service. Depending on the level of the position, salary "bands" can often vary significantly from the low end to the top end.

The goal of the employer is to hire the candidate for the least amount or the amount closest to the low end of the salary band. Companies do this for several reasons:

1. Understand that salaries are typically the highest portion of a department's budget and hiring manager are responsible for staying within their departments overall budget.

2. If the company is able to start a new employee off at a lower salary, they can offer them yearly /merit raises to retain them. This keeps them motivated while staying within the targeted salary range of the position.

3. If a candidate is hired at the top level of the salary band, there is little to no room for any raise. When any employee reaches the top end of a salary band, employers are typically required to change the employee's job description or promote them.

For these reasons, it is very important to learn what the job pays <u>before</u> you reach the interview stage. Learning the positions salary range is often difficult but not impossible. There are several methods to gain a better understanding of what the job will pay:

- Use internet sites such as <u>salary.com,</u> <u>payscale.com</u> and Government sites such as the US Department of Labor site: <u>http://www.bls.gov/oes/current/oes_nat.htm</u> which provides salary comparisons by occupation. Keep in mind that the Governments information may be slightly out of date and usually reflects national salaries versus those that are specific to your geographic area. Researching these sites should provide a reasonable guestimate as to what your type of position should pay.

- Call the company's human resource department and ask what the salary range of the position is. Some HR employees will tell you while others will not.

- Ask network contacts that are current or former employees if they have an idea of what the salary range of the position might be. With their experience and knowledge of what the company pays, they may be able to provide a close guesstimate.

- You may also discuss salary ranges with other network contacts that work in similar functional areas. For example, if you are in finance, you might want to ask other finance types what they believe a finance position with a specific title and function might pay.

Salary vs. Compensation

The benefit of knowing salary information in advance of the interview provides you with the confidence and knowledge to answer any salary questions an interviewer may ask. Most career coaches will recommend that you defer answering salary questions during an interview whenever possible. However, this may not always be possible and if the employer insists, be prepared to answer with a strategy that will leave you room for further negotiation.

For example, if the employer asks about your salary, there are a few ways to strategize in answering these types of question. The first strategy is to attempt to defer answering the question. You can respond by saying; *"While salary is important, at this point I am more concerned as to whether I am a good fit for the position".*

Explain to the interviewer that after they determine that you are the right person for the job, you're confident that you both would be able to come up with an acceptable salary amount.

If pressed for an answer, the second strategy is to capitalize on the differences between *salary* and *compensation*. *Salary* is a fixed amount of money paid to a worker, typically referenced on an annual basis as wages. *Compensation* not only includes salary but also includes all commissions, bonuses, profit sharing, etc. It is the total of all monetary remunerations given to an employee by a company.

A potential strategy to answer a question like *"How much did you make in your last job"* is to respond using your previous *compensation* number instead of your *salary* number. Whether or not you received the compensation incentives in the prior year, your compensation was still the total of all of them. Your salary on the other hand, was only the pay that you actually took home.

So for an example, let's assume your previous salary was $70,000 per year and your compensation plan included a performance bonus and company profit sharing. Assuming your performance bonus was $10,000 and the company profit sharing totaled 5% of your base salary or $3,500, the total compensation for your prior job was $73,500 ($70,000 base salary + $10,000 performance bonus + $3,500 profit sharing). This compensation information may have been given to you in writing as an offer letter or during a performance review.

Therefore, the question could be answered as *"My previous compensation was $73,500."* This was your actual compensation and is a true statement. Never lie or exaggerate about how much you made. This strategy will test whether they are just looking for a number or whether they want to know if they can afford you.

Quite often, the interviewer will write your answer down as a note and move on. If they probe further, be totally honest and explain how your compensation was formulated. Regardless of how deeply the probe, this should improve your negotiating position as they may believe that you will not accept anything less than your prior compensation number as an offer.

From this example, you can see that knowing the salary range is in advance puts you in an better position to respond to the question. Assuming the position has a salary range of $60,000 to $83,000, your answer of $73,500 fits slightly above the median which makes the salary fit within the range. If you are hired with a salary based on your former compensation number, you'll start off with a higher salary than you had before.

Salary Negotiation

When the employer has decided that you are the ideal candidate for the position, there are 3 stages to the process of negotiation. These are; *the initial offer, your counter offer*, and the *final agreement settlement*.

Unless you are working through a recruiter, most negotiations will get resolved within these 3 stages. When negotiating through a recruiter, there maybe one or two more counter offers. By the offer stage, the recruiter wants to ensure you get hired so they can get paid. They will work hard on your behalf to bring the negotiation to a positive conclusion.

The Initial Offer

Once the company has decided to hire you, you'll most likely receive a phone call offering you the position. Even though you are very excited at the prospect of an offer, your response should be positive and upbeat, but not emotional.

Don't accept the offer over the phone. You can respond with something like; *"Thank you very much for selecting me for the position. I am very excited about becoming part of the (COMPANY NAME) team and am looking forward to receiving your offer letter"*.

Always get the offer in writing! Once you receive a written job offer including a salary and benefits spelled out, you will be in a better position to negotiate.

It is important to point out that from the time the employer makes an initial offer until the time you accept the position, you will have the most leverage you will ever have to negotiate.

Many candidates don't even attempt to negotiate because they are afraid they will lose the offer or be rejected. The employer certainly does not want to haggle over salary but if they see you are not totally satisfied or they think you might not accept, they will be more willing to negotiate.

Your Value During the Job Search Process

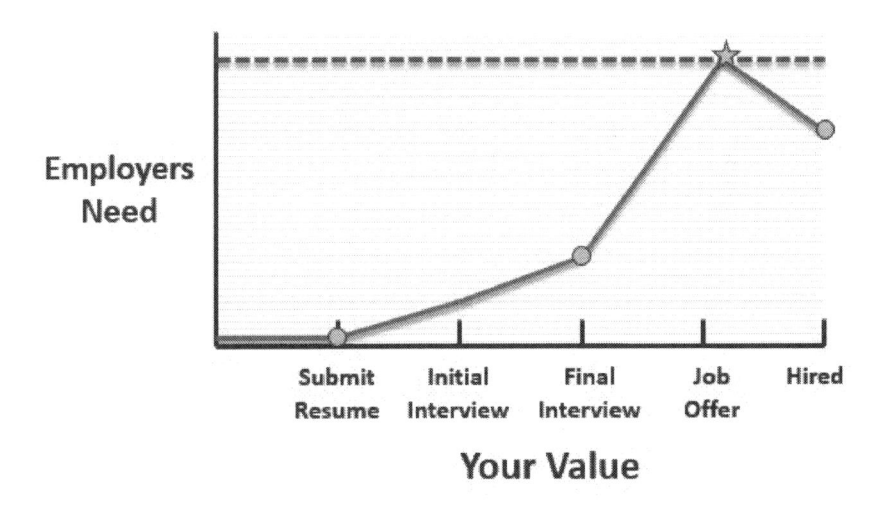

Figure 14-1: Your Value During the Job Search Process

As you can see from the graph above, your ability to negotiate is virtually equal to the employers at the time of the job offer. This reason is; they want you as much as you want the job. From the employer's perspective, they may have been searching several months for the right candidate. During that time, the work has piled up and the last thing they would like to do is start the process all over again with a new batch of candidates. This could happen if you to turn down the position.

Be aware, there is always a danger that there is a "plan B" candidate in the wings just in case you said no or you and the employer cannot come to a mutual hiring agreement. Regardless of whether or not they have a backup candidate, you still have negotiating power when receiving the offer.

Once you accept an offer, you lose your negotiating power. This is the reason why it is so important to get offer details in writing before you accept the offer.

Example 1 – Negotiated Salary Increase

For example, let's say at the time of offer the employer <u>verbally</u> agreed to give you a 5% raise after 6 months. After 6 months have gone by and you remind your manager about the raise, you're shocked when she says, "I don't remember that conversation" or "we agreed to a performance review but not a raise". You have no recourse because you did not have anything in writing.

If your offer letter specifically stated that you were to *"receive a 5% salary increase, 6 months from your start date"*, there would be no question about it and you would be provided with the increase. The lesson here is <u>always get the specifics of an offer in writing before you accept the position</u>.

Example 2 – Negotiate Salary Amount

As another example, let's assume your offer letter contains a $65,000 salary with 2 weeks paid vacation and health insurance. From the salary market research you conducted earlier, you know that the typical salary range for this position is between $64,000 and $80,000 and you are at the low end.

When you receive the offer and it is not as much as you wanted, don't react to let the employer know your concern. Take a few days to consider it, think of what you can negotiate and come back to them with a counter offer. You may want to include other items as part of a more comprehensive package in your counter offer.

The Counter Offer

Always begin the counter offer negotiation with questions. <u>Never issue an ultimatum</u> unless you have another offer in hand. You might say: "Thank you again for the job offer and I am excited about the position. After meeting you, I am confident that we will work very well together. Regarding the salary offer, I was looking for $69,000 per year and I am hoping you could come up to meet that".

If appropriate, you might also share your industry market research to show them that your requested number is at the low end or below average salary for someone with your skills and experience in this type of role. They will be impressed that you did your homework.

However, the employer may have budget limitations, other financial constraints or is just unwilling to compromise. While you are still in the position to accept the offer as is, you might counter with "I understand. Since I am very confident in the contribution I will make for the company, I would like to request that you provide me with a performance review after 90 days and if I meet the agreed to objectives, you will increase my salary by $4,000". If they agree to this, ask that they <u>amend the offer letter to include it in writing</u>.

In your counter offer, ask for several additional items to use as "bargaining chips". In most cases, employers are willing to negotiate with you for these types of non-compensation items. Consider the total package regardless of where the pieces come from. For example, base salary, bonus, car allowance, stock, health insurance and signing bonus, equals a very attractive package.

The following is a listing of potential "bargaining chips" to consider for negotiations. Keep in mind the level of position you apply for will determine what type and how many "bargaining chips" are realistic. (It would be unrealistic to attempt to negotiate for all of them). Prioritize the items which are the most value to your position, lifestyle and career goals. No matter what you negotiate, <u>always</u> request what was agreed to in writing.

Pay and Stock Related Items

- **Signing bonus** – When the employer is not able to meet your salary request at the time of hire, they may be willing to provide a signing bonus for the difference. However, this is a one-time bonus and is not permanent.

- **Performance bonus** – Performance bonuses come in 2 types; guaranteed or discretionary. Guaranteed performance bonuses are paid if the performance goals and metrics are achieved. Discretionary performance bonuses are paid at the discretion of the supervisor or manager, even if the metrics are not met.

- **Promotional increase** – The employer may be willing to negotiate for a predetermined promotion and monetary increase at the time of hire. When an employer locates a strong candidate but doesn't have enough funding to cover the salary for a higher-level position, they may be willing to offer the candidate a lower level position with a planned promotion and increase during the next fiscal year.

- **Company stock** – The employer may be willing to offer company stock as part of a compensation package. Stock is typically issued in non-voting shares with a vesting schedule over several years. Stock is generally offered to the employee at a price below the current market value.

- **Vesting** – In addition to receiving company stock, the company may be willing to expedite the vesting period for the shares. For example, the stock may vest immediately for year 1 or a 4-year vesting schedule may be reduced to 3 years.

- **Equity positions** – When joining a start-up or small company the employer may be willing to negotiate an equity stake in the company. Most equity positions are only offered to upper level or key management candidates. Even if you are at the top, don't expect a huge chunk of the company stock to come your way either. Unless you are negotiating for the President or CEO position, expect the equity stake to be less than 1% of the company stock.

- **Profit sharing** – If the company has a profit sharing program, they will typically include it as part of the initial offer, depending on the level of the position. If they have a profit sharing program but don't present it in the initial offer, it may be something you'll want to negotiate.

- **Commission / percentage** – If you are in sales or in a position that supports sales, you may want to negotiate a commission or some type of incentive percentage of sales based on your contribution or support. Compensation packages for sales reps typically include a base salary plus commission as an incentive.

The ratio of salary to commission varies with the philosophy of each company. Some employers believe sales people should have low pay and high commission (20% base / 80% commission) while others believe the opposite (80% base / 20% commission). There are some that believe in a 50/50 split and others that vary from these including no salary and 100% commission!

- **Guaranteed draw** – For sales and business development positions, salary may include a guaranteed draw. Considering the amount of time and effort that is required to build a client base through new sales, a "draw" is something to consider negotiating at the time of hire. With little to no commission coming in while you build sales, a draw provides a guarantee that you will have regular paycheck with a fixed amount of your salary.

- **Severance package** – While you the employee are in favor at the time of hire, everyone understands you're only as good as the employer perceives you are each year. Generally speaking, higher level management positions are more willing to negotiate severance packages. These packages can include additional income, health insurance, unused vacation, sick leave and stock options which are guaranteed upon termination (assuming termination was not caused by something unlawful or immoral). Severance packages may be regulated by company policy, making them predetermined and leaving you without the ability to negotiate. Do your homework before negotiating severance.

- **Deferred Compensation** – Deferred compensation is an arrangement in which a portion of your income is paid out at a date after which that income is actually earned. Deferred compensation may be provided in the form of pensions, retirement plans, and stock options. However, the primary benefit of negotiating deferred compensation is to defer a tax liability if your personal financial situation requires this.

- **Early Retirement** – Depending on how valuable you are to the company and your age, you may be able to negotiate an early retirement package.

Health / Insurance Related Items

- **Immediate Insurance Coverage** – Generally speaking, new employees do not receive insurance coverage during a new employee "evaluation" period. (e.g. the first 90 days). The amount of time the evaluation period lasts varies by company, but obtaining immediate insurance is usually an easily negotiated benefit. This assumes the company does not have a firm policy against making exceptions for insurance. In addition to health insurance, other insurance benefits may include life, dental and/ or eye care.

- **Health Club Membership** – The employer may be willing to pay for your membership to a health club. Healthy employees have less sick days so this is also a long-term benefit for the employer. Companies may also have negotiated discounted rates for specific health club memberships.

- **Family Sick Leave** – If you have a parent or family member that is poor health, you may want to negotiate for sick leave. I don't recommend discussing the details of your personal situation, but ask for the sick leave when you are negotiating the offer.

- **Maternity Leave** – If you are planning to or have become pregnant, this is a good time to negotiate the amount of maternity leave that you may require. The company most likely has a policy in place (under State or Federal law) but you may be able to negotiate an extended period of maternity leave.

Travel Related Benefits

- **Car Allowance / Car** – If you're in management or in a position that requires territory travel by car, negotiate for a company car or at least for a car allowance. At minimum, negotiate for fuel reimbursement. Wear and tear on your personal vehicle may be more expensive than you realize so any type of vehicle benefit will offset your personal costs.

- **Cell Phone** – If your position requires travel or the ability to communicate past normal working hours, request that the company provide you with a cell phone or at minimum, reimburse you for your business related cell phone charges.

- **Expense Account** – If your job requires interaction with customers (sales/ business development), you may negotiate for an entertainment expense account. Clients usually expect you to pick up the check and it would be costly if it's out of your own pocket.

- **Company Credit Cards** – If your position requires travel or is a job that involves purchasing expensive items for the company, you'll want to consider negotiating for a company credit card. It is to your advantage to have one. For example, if you are the marketing tradeshow coordinator, you may be required to purchase numerous expensive rental items for a single tradeshow event. Having a company credit card ensures that your personal credit does not get damaged from late payments if your employer is late reimbursing you for the expense.

- **Meals** – Companies typically pay for meals for those that travel. If they do not, you will want to negotiate to have the company pay for your meals while on the road. Depending on your commute or work hours, it may be impractical to get home in time for dinner so you may want to negotiate having the company pay for meals during the work week.

- **Business or 1st Class Airline Tickets** – If your position requires that you fly long distances of more than 5 or 6 hours, getting the company to upgrade your class of travel seating may be something you'll want to negotiate.

- **Travel Benefits** – For the frequent flyer, you may want to negotiate for air lounge memberships (priority pass, red carpet room, admirals club, etc.), travel insurance and / or the use of limo services to and from the airport.

- **Ride Sharing Programs** – If your company is located far away from your home or there is limited parking at the work site, you might consider negotiating for a ride share program to improve your commute to and from work by utilizing a shared vehicle.

Recreation / Time off Related

- **Vacation Time** – Most companies offer 2 weeks paid vacation and the ability to accrue additional time off with years of service. Requesting an extra week is a negotiable benefit unless the company has a fixed firm policy that applies to all employees. You would be surprised how often a request for an additional week is granted.

- **National or Personal Holidays** – In addition to your vacation, you may want to negotiate for National or personal holidays. For example, if you work for a defense company, they may consider your request for National patriotic holidays in addition to those they already provide.

- **Company Sponsored Events / Charity Matching** – If you are involved in a community organization or charity that you are passionate about, you may want to negotiate for the company's sponsorship or charitable contribution to that organization or event.

Personal Benefits

- **Telecommuting** – With today's technology, working from home has become far more acceptable by employers. If you have small children or a long commute, you may want to consider asking to allow you to work from home 1 or 2 days a week.

- **Parking Places or Permits** – Quite often, management positions will provide a dedicated parking space for your vehicle. If they do not, you may consider negotiating for one.

- **Job Sharing** – If you have the responsibility of taking care of family members with illnesses, have small children or a long commute, you may want to consider negotiating to share your job with another employee. This allows both employees to have greater flexibility and still have the ability to work.

- **Legal / Financial Accounting Services** – If your personal situation requires that you need legal or financial help with a tax return, will preparation or estate planning, you might consider asking the company to pay for the expense.

- **Product / Service Discounts** – If your new company makes products that you would like to purchase, you might negotiate a fixed discount on their products or services.

Dues and Memberships

- **Organizational Dues** – As part of your new position, you may want to join one or more industry related trade organizations. Ask the company to consider paying your membership dues.

- **Club Memberships** - If your job requires interaction with customers or industry leaders, you may want to negotiate for memberships to golf or other types of private clubs for entertainment and to discuss business.

- **Magazine or On-line Subscriptions** – To keep up on the latest trends in your industry, you might consider requesting that the company pay for industry related publications and /or subscriptions. For example, if you are a graphic artist, you might subscribe to a service that provides downloadable photos or images on-line.

- **Event Tickets** – If your job requires interaction with customers, you may want to negotiate for season tickets to one or more of the professional home sports teams or other venues to entertain clients.

Education Related

- **Child Care Programs** - If you have small children at home, you may want to consider asking the company to pay for child care while you are at work or offer company sponsored child care programs.

- **Scholarships** - If you have children that are about to enter college or already in college, you may want to consider asking the company to pay a portion of their tuition as a company sponsored scholarship.

There were many suggestions provided that could be part of a potential compensation package. During the counter offer, know which of these you want to negotiate tempered by what you think you can actually get. You have a short window of time to do your negotiating as the employer wants this to come to closure quickly.

The Final Agreement

One other important thing to recognize is when to stop negotiating with the employer. Listen carefully to how they react to your requests and stop if the conversation gets cumbersome or uncomfortable. Finally, I cannot emphasize enough the importance of getting the details spelled out in a written offer once you reach a final agreement.

Like any new skill, negotiating may seem somewhat awkward at first so it's a good idea to practice with a friend. Focus on answering salary questions and how you would negotiate other benefits. Be sure to practice this with others before you actually negotiate with the employer. Learn to negotiate like a pro and reap the rewards!

Best of luck in your job search!

ABOUT THE AUTHOR

Gary Calvaneso is a retired corporate executive with over 30 years of global sales and marketing experience. His executive leadership includes experience with some of the world's most respected medical device, computer technology, aerospace and defense companies.

He has a proven track record of building business through recruiting and hiring the right top talent. Gary has considerable personal experience in understanding what it takes to change careers and rise to the top of an organization.

For nearly 9 years, Gary participated as volunteer member of Saddleback Church's Career Coaching and Counseling Ministry. As a Career Coaching member, he has served as the leader of curriculum development, designing the course materials and teaching thousands of people the job seeking skills needed to be successful.

During his career, Gary also served as an advisor to ABC news, Frost & Sullivan and has written articles for a number of industry magazines.